THE Drum Recording HANDBOOK

To access online media visit:
www.halleonard.com/mylibrary
Enter code:

8513-8785-2055-8525

THE Drum Recording HANDBOOK

music PRO guides

THE Drum Recording HANDBOOK

Second Edition

Bobby Owsinski and Dennis Moody

Hal Leonard Books
An Imprint of Hal Leonard Corporation

Second edition published in 2016 by Hal Leonard Books

An Imprint of Hal Leonard Corporation
7777 West Bluemound Road
Milwaukee, WI 53213

Trade Book Division Editorial Offices
33 Plymouth St., Montclair, NJ 07042

First edition published in 2008 by Hal Leonard Books

All illustrations by Bobby Owsinski except the following: 1-2 from Remo Inc.; 3-1 from Vic Firth Company; 3-2 from Behringer; 3-3 from Hear Technologies; 5-8 from Yamaha Corporation of America; 5-10 from Drum Workshop, Inc.; 5-11 from The X Clip; 8-1 from RTOM, Inc.

Printed in the United States of America

Book design by John J. Flannery

Library of Congress Cataloging-in-Publication Data

Names: Owsinski, Bobby. | Moody, Dennis.
Title: The drum recording handbook / Bobby Owsinski and Dennis Moody.
Description: Second edition. | Milwaukee, WI : Hal Leonard Books, 2016. |
  Series: Music pro guides | Includes index.
Identifiers: LCCN 2015050753 | ISBN 9781495045240 (pbk.)
Subjects: LCSH: Drum set. | Sound–Recording and reproducing.
Classification: LCC MT662 .O97 2016 | DDC 786.9/149–dc23
LC record available at http://lccn.loc.gov/2015050753

ISBN: 978-1-4950-4524-0

www.halleonardbooks.com

CONTENTS

INTRODUCTION

Many young musicians and recording engineers have the mistaken impression that all you need to do is throw some microphones on a drum kit and it will automatically sound pretty good. This may be because there are a few superstar engineers who make it look so darned easy, or it may be because of the many books, articles, and websites that churn out the same info to the point where it feels like gospel.

But getting good drum sounds is as much of an art as it is a craft. Sure, it takes good ears (everything in music does), but it also takes a lot of knowledge about why drums sound good in the first place.

> *. . . a lot of engineers cannot capture what a real acoustic drum set sounds like.*
>
> —Ricky Lawson

> *. . . even 57s on the toms can sound OK with the right engineer.*
>
> —Johnny "Vatos" Hernandez

And that's the reason why we put so much more into this book than the simple "place the mic here" kind of information. The more you know about the drums themselves, the more you know why the kit you're working with sounds good, or bad. The more you know about how real honest-to-God session drummers think and work, the more you're able to accommodate the drummer who's setting up for you to record right now.

If you happen to be a drummer, the more you know about your kit and what's expected of you in the studio, the better you'll be able to sound and perform.

> *. . . it's all a combination of drum heads and microphones and processing and the engineer to make things sound good. You can have a $10,000 drum kit and he can make things sound like cracker boxes, and you can have cracker boxes and he can make it sound like a $10,000 kit.*
>
> —Ricky Lawson

We packed in as much information about all aspects of getting drum sounds as we could in the book and the online videos, because in order to recognize when you have something that's really great, you have to know what to look for first.

I'm telling you that the sound is in the engineering and the studio environment. It's not really what I like to see on the drums, it's who I see engineering because you can get a cat that doesn't know what he's doing and it can be a nightmare. Back in the day, they might have only used three or four mics tops, but if a guy knew what he was doing he got a killer drum sound. It's the engineering factor that plays such a big part in the situation.

—Ricky Lawson

FROM BOBBY OWSINSKI

There are a lot of books and courses that give you tips on drum miking, but they always approach it from the standpoint of a pro, outlining the high-end microphones, signal path, and acoustically correct studio that usually only pros have access to. This approach is certainly useful as it's great to try to emulate what these guys are doing, but it can also be a bit impractical if you just don't have the means or access to the room and gear that's usually described.

This book takes a different approach. It assumes that you don't have the resources of a pro. It assumes that you just have the barest of recording essentials to get the job done. It assumes that you only have a minimum of gear like most people just starting out, because in the end, none of that matters. There's a lot more to getting a drum sound than the gear you use, and that's what you'll discover herein.

Even though I engineer myself, Dennis Moody has always been my go-to guy when I produce a project. It's really difficult for me to both engineer and produce in the heat of battle, so to speak, and Dennis and I have always worked well together. He gets great sounds quickly and easily and I'm left to concentrate on my job since he does such a great job at his.

And drum sounds have always been his specialty. While other engineers might struggle for hours (and once upon a time when budgets were big, even days) trying to get a kit to sound reasonably good, Dennis has a knack for making a kit sound like something Zeus is playing on Mt. Olympus (that means it sounds great!) in such a short amount of time that it makes you wonder how anyone can be that efficient.

That's exactly what this book will teach you—how to make just about any kit record so well that you'll be shocked, and all without a lot of expensive equipment.

FROM DENNIS MOODY

No matter what type of music you're preparing to record, getting a good drum sound is the foundation of a good recording project. Whether you're a drummer wanting to test out your new DAW or an aspiring sound engineer recording a band for the first time, trying to mike a drum kit and getting a halfway decent sound can seem not just intimidating, but completely overwhelming.

I'm an audio engineer who's worked with most of the top drummers in the world, but I can still recall when I began trying to record on my own. I remember the first time I walked into a professional studio and the awkwardness of not knowing my way around. I also think back to the first time I assisted an engineer and how he made everything look so easy, but I only had a vague idea as to what he was doing.

Every session that I did on my own in those early days, I remember wishing that I had an experienced sound engineer with me who could take the time to answer my questions and save me the frustration of trying to figure things out, so I could get on with the fun of recording. Well, this book is the next best thing to having me with you to answer your questions.

We've broken down the basics of recording drums into a very simple, step-by-step process and put this into an easy-to-bring-to-the-studio book that you can refer to as you set up your projects. In this book, you'll learn not only the miking techniques, but what you need to do to prepare to record a killer drum track.

There are so many subtleties to drum miking that, in the long run, your best teacher is going to be trial and error. But the more you are willing to experiment, the more you will learn, and today's the day you start your education. Don't be afraid to dive right in and start recording. Sure, you're bound to get some "interesting" sounds along the way, but you won't be the first. I've seen even legendary engineers make recording mistakes when it comes to drums.

However, there are basics that everyone trying to record drums should know, and that will be the starting point for your own experimentation. With the tips you get in this book, you'll feel more confident around the studio, whether it's a simple home four-track or a professional multi-track recording studio. By utilizing this book, you are well on your way to getting the drums recorded exactly as you hear them in your head.

I've often been asked to recommend the best equipment for recording, from drum heads to mics, to acoustics. At the top of each section, we've included a list of equipment that will probably be needed to complete the steps in that section (besides the basics, such as console or mic preamps, mic cables, and the like), as well as a list of popular brands that are commonly used. You don't necessarily need these specific brands to get the job done, but if you're in the market to purchase new equipment and want to know what will serve the purpose well, then this list will save you lots of money otherwise spent on "junk" that won't do the job with the ease and quality that you'll eventually want.

Not everyone has an unlimited budget, so we've picked the most popular in three price categories:

Industry Standard: A choice that you'll see used the majority of the time.

Popular Alternative: Often used alternative mic choices.

Inexpensive Substitute: A workhorse that will get the job done but won't break your budget.

I encourage you to use the information you find in this book as a springboard. Try the different suggestions we offer until you find the individual sound you want to hear, and always take detailed notes so that you can reproduce that same effect the next time you record. As the recording engineer, you too are an artist, and each engineer has different preferences, likes and dislikes—in a word, style—and experimentation is the key to developing that style.

Always remember the ultimate rule in recording: "What you hear is what you get." If you like what you hear, it is irrelevant how you got it to sound that way. That's what experimentation is all about.

Be creative, and most of all, have fun!!

MEET THE DRUMMERS

We thought that it was really important that you heard about drums, drum tuning, and drum miking from the drummer's point of view, so we interviewed seven of the music industry's very best. You'll find that hearing about getting a great drum recording from their perspective is very enlightening. Their full interviews are included in the final part of the book (Michael White is on the online videos), but you'll see quotes from the interviews mixed throughout the book wherever they might be appropriate.

Bernie Dresel is widely recognized for his fifteen years with The Brian Setzer Orchestra, but he now does a variety of studio work that goes anywhere from the television shows like *The Simpsons* and *Family Guy*, to movies like *Speed Racer*, to the blues-rock of Carl Verheyen, to the big band sound of Gordon Goodwin's Big Phat Band, to R&B icons like Chaka Khan and Patti LaBelle.

The heartbeat of the band Oingo Boingo for seventeen years, **Johnny "Vatos" Hernandez** has gone on to use his widely diverse background to play on a variety of movies, television shows (*Battlestar Galactica*) and commercials (Tostitos, Honda, Kia, Chrysler) as well as a wide variety of musical and orchestral gigs in all sorts of styles.

It just might be easier to say who **Ricky Lawson** hasn't played with rather than who he has. Unfortunately, Ricky passed away before the latest version of this book was published, but his interview is still as valuable as ever. Having performed with Quincy Jones, the Brothers Johnson, Phil Collins, Steely Dan, Eric Clapton, Babyface, Lionel Ritchie, Anita Baker (*Rapture*), Whitney Houston ("I Will Always Love You"), and, as musical director for Michael Jackson, Ricky was also the original drummer for Yellowjackets when he won best R&B Instrumental Grammy in 1987 ("And You Know That," the first track from the album *Shades*). There's obviously a reason why these musical giants had him on a first-call basis: not only was he massively talented but exceedingly humble—and helpful to others as well.

Brian MacLeod has been one of the most in-demand session drummers in L.A. for quite some time now, and with good reason. Brian has the ability to make tracks feel not just pretty good, but awesomely great. Just listen to the groove in Sheryl Crow's breakthrough hit "All I Wanna Do" and you'll hear exactly what Brian is known for. If you're a fan of the television shows *The Office* or *Dirty Sexy Money*, that's him playing on the theme songs. Add to this, his recordings for

Christina Aguilera, Madonna, Chris Isaac, John Hiatt, Tears for Fears, Jewel, and many, many others, and you get the picture of just why the Brian MacLeod touch is so sought after.

Kellii Scott has played with the alternative rock band Failure off and on for more than twenty years. In between, he was a member of producer/ songwriter Linda Perry's house band, working on projects with Christina Aguilera, Pink, Faith Hill, Hole, Scissor Sisters, and many others.

Dave Weckl is truly one of the most widely respected drummers in the drumming world. From his early days with Chick Corea's Elektric Band, to touring with the likes of Simon and Garfunkel and Mike Stern, to playing on numerous radio and television jingles and soundtracks, to sessions with Robert Plant, George Benson, and Peabo Bryson (among many others), to being a highly regarded solo artist in his own right, Dave has always been recognized as a cutting-edge innovator of his instrument. Dave is also a consummate educator, with many instructional videos/DVDs and play-along packages to his credit. You can learn a lot more about Dave and his instructional products at daveweckl.com.

Michael White has played with everyone from Earth, Wind & Fire; Steely Dan; the Commodores; Al Jarraeu; Curtis Mayfield; Whitney Houston; Frankie Beverly and Maze; and countless others. Michael's playing and tuning techniques are featured on the videos at DrumRecordingHandbook.com.

CHAPTER ONE
THE DRUM KIT

The most important part of getting a good drum sound is having the drums sound great in the room even before you touch a microphone. This sound can be elusive, as sometimes even good drummers don't know how to properly tune their drums, so here's a quick look at what it takes to make the sound of the drum kit rock in the room.

Engineer's Drum Kit Checklist:

✓ New heads
✓ Duct or gaffers tape (for keeping hardware in place)
✓ Moongel or dampening ring (for getting rid of rings)
✓ WD-40 (for getting squeaks out of hardware)
✓ Sound baffles (for isolation from other instruments)
✓ Throw rug (large enough for the drums to fit on)
✓ Tuning key (two keys make tuning faster)
✓ Paper towels (for getting rid of rings)
✓ Light packing blanket (for dampening the kick drum)
✓ Heavy packing blanket (for isolating the kick mic, if needed)
✓ Board tape (for marking mic and stand placement)
✓ Sharpie (for marking mic and stand placement)

WHAT MAKES A KIT SOUND GREAT?

While the definition of *great* is different to different people on a general level, in the studio it usually means a kit that's well-tuned and free of buzzes and sympathetic vibrations. This means that when you hit the rack tom, for instance, the snare doesn't buzz and the other toms don't ring along with it. If you hit the snare, the toms don't ring along.

So how do you achieve this drum nirvana? It's all in the tuning and the kit maintenance, which we'll check out in depth later in the chapter. First, let's take a look at drum construction itself, since it helps to have a little background in why drums sound the way they do so that you can determine just what a drum kit is capable of.

Drum Construction

There are a number of parameters that determine what a drum will sound like. Let's take a look at them.

Shell Size

The diameter of a drum has the most impact on the natural pitch of a drum. The larger the diameter, the lower the natural pitch, although you can obviously change this by tuning the heads.

Shell Depth

While the shell depth does contribute to the tone, it's mostly responsible for how loud the drum will be and, to some degree, the articulation of the sound. This means that a shallow shell (like a 9" tom) doesn't have as much surface area as a larger one, so the sound is a bit shorter, with a sharper attack. A drum with more depth (like a 12" tom) will have a lower resonant frequency, so the attack will be a bit longer and warmer and the drum will be louder.

Shell Thickness

Shell thickness is usually overlooked as a contributing factor to the sound of a drum. Thinner shells are actually more resonant since they're easier to excite. That's because they have a lower mass than a heavier, thicker shell. As a result, thicker shells have to rely much more on the heads for the overall tone of the drum.

Shell Material

Probably out of all the parameters described here, the material used to make the drum shell is most responsible for the tone of the drums. Here are the most commonly found drum shell materials.

- **Maple**. Generally speaking, maple is the most prized construction material by drummers, primarily because the sound is so even across the drum frequency spectrum. It's expensive and becoming more difficult to find since it's a slow growth tree.
- **Mahogany** is another slow growth tree that is becoming increas-

ingly hard to find. True U.S. or Honduran mahogany is considered the best, but other woods from the Philippines, Southeast Asia, China, and Malaysia are sometimes labeled as mahogany simply because they have the same look as the U.S. or Honduran wood. The problem is, they don't sound the same since their density varies from the real thing. Mahogany drums sound warmer than maple since the low end is increased.

- **Birch** is a very dense wood, which, thanks to its hardness, results in a brighter drum with a lot less low end than maple.
- **Poplar** is a fast growing tree, which translates into cheaper wood and inexpensive drum kits. It has a sound very similar to birch, with a bright top end and less bottom.
- **Basswood** is also a fast growing tree, resulting in inexpensive kits, but exhibits an increased low end that's similar to mahogany.
- **Luaan** is an Asian tree that provides the least expensive wood available. It's strong and is easy to stain, so it generally looks good. It also has a warmer sound with less top end, similar to mahogany.

Shell Interior

Although it's not widely known, the interior of the drum shell has a lot to do with the pitch of the drum. A rough interior produces a less resonant drum, since the roughness breaks up the interior reflections. A smooth interior results in a more resonant drum, which means it's easier to tune and control.

Bearing Edges

Maybe the least understood aspect of giving a drum its tone is the bearing edges of the shell (the cut at the edge of a drum shell where the hoops are attached). The way the bearing edge is cut not only affects the pitch of the drum, but the tuning as well. The sharper the cut, the brighter the sound.

The degree at which the edge is cut makes all the difference in the sound of the drum. A sharp 45° angled cut will result in a long sustain with bright overtones. A 30° cut will provide less of a high-pitched ring. Rounded edges produce a muted, poorer tone. All bearing edges must be flat and true with the exact same degree of cut. For more on bearing edges, see the tips from the Drum Doctor later in this chapter.

Hoops

The type of hoop and the number of lugs used to seat the drum heads also determines how the drum will sound. In general, the thicker the hoop, the easier the drum will be to tune. Fewer lugs provide more complex overtones.

Stamped hoops are made from a variety of metals, all of which affect the tone a bit differently, but most drummers feel they get a warmer tone from die cast hoops. Aluminum gives a high pitch while brass provides more overtones.

Die cast hoops are generally both thicker and stronger than stamped hoops, so the drum becomes easier to tune. There are fewer overtones as a byproduct.

Wood hoops come in different thicknesses, so they can be made to sound like either a stamped or a cast hoop, only brighter.

A LOOK AT THE SNARE

Since the snare is the most important drum in the kit, it's best we take a look at it on its own since there are so many other factors that influence the tone besides what we just discussed.

Snare Construction

There are a lot of other materials used for snare drums, but first, here are a couple of things to consider:

- **Metal snare drums are generally very loud, resonant, and bright.** The thickness really makes a difference, with 3mm and thicker having more low end and midrange.
- **The stand can affect the sound.** If it's wrapped too tightly around the drum it will decrease its vibration, causing the sound to be more muted with fewer overtones.

The Snare Unit

Another important aspect is the snare unit itself. The snare count, type of material, curl, and diameter all determine the volume of the snare as well as any sympathetic vibrations that may occur.

Make sure the snare unit is flat against the head, and that there are no sharp or uneven protrusions. Less curl will mean less volume while a wider snare unit will have more volume. Too much snare volume, however, will mean that the snare is hard to control when other drums are hit.

TUNING THE DRUMS

Nothing beats the sound of a well-tuned drum kit, especially one that's been tuned specifically for the studio. Here are some steps to take to tune that kit.

Step 1: Secure the Drums

It's a good idea to set up the drums on a small throw rug so they don't slide around while they're being played. If you don't have a rug or happen to like the sound of the reflections from the floor, some drummers use duct tape to secure the kit (or even nail it) to the floor. (Make sure you get permission from the studio before trying that, though, unless you also happen to be a professional floor refinisher.)

Step 2: Replace the Heads

There's nothing like a new drum head to give the drum a great tone. Many engineers prefer the sound of thinner heads, such as Remo's Diplomat, FD, and Thin/FD lines for recording, but the disadvantage of these is that they tend to wear out more quickly. A general-duty head, such as Remo's Ambassador line, lasts longer and, if new, should sound nearly as good.

For recording purposes, it's sometimes best to avoid heavy-duty heads, such as Remo's Emperor, PinStripe, PowerStroke, and the Black, Clear, or White Dot series. These are all great heads, but they're designed more for live performance and tend to constrict the sound a bit, making the drum a bit flat sounding instead of bright and exciting. Save yourself some studio time and mixing grief by getting a separate set of heads for recording and saving the extra-thick heads for gigs.

I just kind of move the combination of drum heads around to get different things. If I want a heavier sound, I'll use a thicker head. If I want it brighter with more attack, I'll use a thinner head. I usually don't go any thinner than an Ambassador and I usually don't go any thicker than an Emperor.

— Ricky Lawson

Step 3: Head Configuration

There are a lot of choices when it comes to how a drummer personalizes the sound of his kit. Some approaches lend themselves to a better studio sound than others, however.

For example, should the tom-toms have a bottom head or not? In the late 1970s and early '80s, it was the "style of the day" to use a tom with only a top head and have the bottom head removed. Having both heads on does require a bit more tuning time, though, since it's important to tune both of them. Try it both ways and decide which one helps you achieve the right sound for the song.

Step 4: Mute the Rattles

If there are any audible rings or rattles when you stand in front of the drum kit while the drummer is playing, the mics will surely hear them too. Use some WD-40 to eliminate any squeaks coming from the bass drum or hi-hat pedals, unless you're trying to replicate John Bonham's squeaky pedal in "Houses of the Holy."

Step 5: Tuning the Snare Drum

A key component to getting a great drum sound is getting the snare to sound right for the music. This is the point where you get to make some artistic decisions. Does the song call for a deep, rich, low-tuned snare or a higher-pitched, tight, *crack!* tuning? Do you want a more open, ringing tone or a deadened, heavy thud?

Most jazz drummers have a more open sound as compared to dance music, which tends to have a deader sound. In rock music you can find examples of almost every snare tone imaginable.

To get that flat, thudding sound, try placing a 4" (13 cm) piece of duct tape on the top head in a spot where it won't get hit by the drummer. Usually this means on the top part of the head next to the rim. Tape down a wad of paper towels or tissue paper to deaden the drums, but be careful not to overdo it and deaden it too much (see Figure 1-1).

I'm not afraid to tape up my kit if I need to get it to fit better with the song, though, because you have to tune your drums for the microphones. Sometimes the drum kit might not sound good in the room after you tune it, but it might sound amazing when you play it back. This can be very deceiving for young kids especially. A young drummer might have his kit tuned so they sound just wonderful

live, but you tune it differently for recording. Sometimes I'll use tons of duct tape. I'm not afraid to tape up drums or pad them down to get a nice tight sound if that's what the producer is looking for.
— Brian MacLeod

I don't think it's good to tune the snare drum on the snare stand. It's better on a table or floor so it's laying flat. You make sure you get your head on flat if you have to change one, then tighten each lug so that it's barely touching the rim, then just finger tighten the lugs (crisscrossing as you go) so you make sure that you don't over-tighten one. At that point you can start using the drum key.
— Bernie Dresel

Figure 1-1: Using a wad of paper towel and duct tape to deaden the snare.

There's also a new device from Remo that Dave Weckl helped design called the Active Snare Dampening System, which goes a long way to eliminating the need to tape up your snare to get rid of any unwanted ringing (see Figure 1-2).

Figure 1-2: The Remo Active Snare Dampening System.

Once fitted to the drum by attaching it to the rim, you can adjust the amount of dampening by either moving the dampener from the center to the edge of the drum head, or by sliding the O-ring up or down.

Remember, when it comes to deadening, a little goes a very long way. What may seem like a moderate amount of dampening might make your drums sound like cardboard boxes. That may be the sound you're looking for, but know that it doesn't take a lot to get there.

Tips to Reduce Snare Buzzing

One of the attributes to a well-tuned kit is the fact that there's not much snare ring when you hit the other drums. Obviously this should be one of the main goals when tuning your kit, since it makes the whole kit sound way better. Here are a few tricks to help prevent those unwanted sympathetic vibrations.

- Tune the snare-side head to a different pitch.
- Tune the batter head of the snare to a different pitch.

There's a lot of different theories about how a drum should sound, but the one that works best for me is when the top head is not exactly the same pitch as the bottom. The top head I tune about a minor third above the bottom head when you're just barely tapping it right on the edge near the lug.

—Bernie Dresel

- Detune the lugs on either side of one or both ends of the snares (on the snare-side head). This, in effect, makes the snare-side head out of tune, so its resonant frequency won't be as strong. If you want to refine this a bit, detune both lugs on either side of the snare where it attaches to the shell until the head ripples on the snare side of a ten-lug snare with a stamped hoop. Tune it back up until the ripple just disappears.
- This means you will have detuned four lugs. Now, compensate by over-tightening the remaining six lugs (three on either side of the snares). This results in the head being tightened only in the middle of the snares.
- The worst area for snare buzz is the place on the snare where the steel plate is soldered to the wires. It has a small gap that causes most of the offensive buzzes. If the snare head around this area is completely detuned, there'll be no buzz!
- You'll notice that the drum now looks out of round on the bottom, but it's not. That's because only the snare side rim is bent. The bendability of a triple stamped hoop is the reason why it's so accurate for tuning.
- Tune the offending tom to a different pitch.

. . . I'm so hyper-sensitive to hitting a drum and have another one ring. All that crosstalk crap has got to go.

—Johnny "Vatos" Hernandez

Step 6: Tune the Drums

Speaking of tuning, the heads are tuned to the desired pitch, which is different for every drummer and drum kit. There are some tuning tips and tricks in the next section.

So what I try to do between my three toms, the 12", 14", and 16", is to have them maybe a fourth apart in pitch and that way you don't get an octave between the highest tom and the lowest and they sound musical together. Now if you have a lot of toms then maybe tuning them a major third apart could work, but with three toms I think a fourth is good because all three are tuned within the same octave and a fifth is too much because they're not.

—Bernie Dresel

I tap the side of the shell to see how it will sound in the room, then I tune it accordingly so that the drum is working at its maximum value in relation to the room. I do that everywhere I go, whether it's a ballroom or a wedding or Studio D at Village Recorders or Conway [famous Hollywood recording studios], or the House of Blues or the Gibson Amphitheater. I always tune the drums for the room. My idea of a good-sounding drum is when you can just throw a mic in front of it and it works without any EQ or processing, which engineers love.

—Johnny "Vatos" Hernandez

What I try to do is to tune to where the drum sounds good. You can take a drum and you can tune it out of the range of what it likes to be in, so I just try to find the sweet spot for that drum with the combination of heads that I'm using. I like the top head a little bit tighter and then I use the bottom head just to bring in some tone.

—Ricky Lawson

TUNING TIPS FROM THE DRUM DOCTOR

If you're doing a session in Los Angeles and you want your drums to instantly sound great, then your first call is to the Drum Doctors, to either rent a fantastic sounding kit or have your kit tuned. Ross Garfield is the "Drum Doctor" and you've heard his drum sounds on platinum recordings from Alanis Morissette, the Black Crowes, Bruce Springsteen, Rod Stewart, Metallica, the Rolling Stones, Marilyn Manson, Dwight Yoakam, Jane's Addiction, Red Hot Chili Peppers, Foo Fighters, Lenny Kravitz, Michael Jackson, Rage Against the Machine, Sheryl Crow, and Nirvana, among many others.

Not many people know as much about drums and drum tuning as Ross, as the following tips were discovered after years of working closely with the likes of drumming greats Jeff Porcaro, Jim Keltner, Charlie Watts, Terry Bozzio, Jeff Hamilton, Steve Jordan, Charlie

Drayton, and Peter Erskine (to name just a few). You can also find out more about the Drum Doctors at www.drumdoctors.com.

Big Drums vs. Small Drums

Ross Garfield: "What's important is to have the right size drums for the song. If you're going for that big double-headed Bonham sound, you really should have a 26" kick drum. If you're going for a Jeff Porcaro punchy track like 'Rosanna,' then you should probably have a 22", but, ultimately, the music will determine the drum sound you need—maybe not so much the drums themselves, but definitely the tuning.

"For instance, the drums that I bring for a hip-hop session are actually very close to what I bring for a jazz session. Usually the hip-hop guys want a little bass drum like an 18", and an 18" or a 20" kick is what's common for a jazz session. A hip-hop session will use maybe a 12" or a 14" rack tom, which is also similar to the jazz setup.

"The big difference is in the snare and hi-hats and the tuning of the kick drum and the snare. On a jazz session I would keep the kick drum tuned high and probably not muffled. On a hip-hop session I would tune the kick probably as low as it would go and definitely not have any muffling so it has as big a *boom* as I can get.

"I would also bring a selection of snares from like a 4"x12" snare, 3"x13" and maybe a 3"x14". On a jazz record I'd probably bring a 5"x14" and a 6.5"x14". The hi-hats on a jazz record would almost definitely be 14s, where [on] a hip-hop record you'd want a pair of 10s or 12s, or maybe even 13s. Of course, none of this is written in stone because I'm sure a lot of hip-hop records have been made with bigger sets."

How Long Does It Take to Tune a Drum Kit?

Ross Garfield: "If I have to change all the heads and tune them up, it'll take about an hour before we can start listening through the microphones, and that's even on a cheap starter set.

"I try to tune them to where I think they should be, a little on the high side for starters, then after we open up the mics and hear everything magnified, I'll modify the tuning more to the song."

Prepping the Drums for New Heads

Ross Garfield: "In order for drums to sound their best, the edges of the drum shell have to be cut properly, and this is something that no one ever checks, or even thinks of checking, until it's time to change the heads.

"When you take the heads off, all the edges of the shell should lie exactly flat against a flat surface. I'll put the shell on a piece of glass or granite and shine a light over the top of the shell, then I'll get down to where the edge of the drum hits the granite. If I see a light at any point then there's a low spot on the edge of the shell, and the drum will be hard to tune and probably have some funny overtones.

"That said, the first thing is to make sure that your drum shells are true. The next thing is for your shell edge to have a bevel to it, and not be flat on the bottom, because again, this affects the tuning and overtones.

"If you have either of these problems with a drum, send it back to the manufacturer. Don't try to cut the edges of your drum shells yourself since it doesn't cost that much money for the manufacturer to do it and it's really something that should be done by someone who knows exactly what they're doing. Once your drum shells are in good shape, then tuning is a lot easier."

New Heads

Ross Garfield: "The first thing I'll do is put a fresh set of top and bottom heads on. Nine times out of ten, I'll put white Remo Ambassadors on the tops, clear Remo Ambassadors on the bottoms, and a Remo clear Powerstroke 3 on the kick drum. I'll use a white Ambassador or a coated black dot Ambassador on the snare top and either a clear Diplomat or coated Ambassador on the bottom.

"A lot of the decision on the type of head depends on how deep the drum is. If it's 5" or less I'll usually go with an Ambassador, and if it's 6 1/2" or bigger I'll usually go with a Diplomat. Just this little bit of information really makes a difference in how the kit sounds.

"A heavy hitter will get more low end out of a drum that's tuned higher just because of the way he hits, so as a result I usually tune a drum a little tighter if the drummer is a heavy hitter. I might move into different heads as well, like an Emperor or something thicker."

The Tuning Technique

Ross Garfield: "Most engineers (and even a lot of drummers) don't know the proper way to tune their drums, but it's really not that hard. For a proper tune job, you've got to keep all of the tension rods even so they have the same tension at each lug.

"You hit the head an inch in front of the lug, and if you do it enough times you'll hear which ones are higher and which are lower.

What you want is for the pitch to sound the same at each lug. When the pitch (the tension) is the same at each lug, then when you hit the drum in the center you should have a nice even decay.

"Tune the top and the bottom head to the same pitch at first, then take the bottom head down a third to a fifth below the top head."

Should the Drums Be Tuned to the Key of the Song?

Ross Garfield: "Usually I just tune the kit so it sounds good with the key of the song rather than in-pitch with it, because if one of the other players hits the same note that the snare or kick is tuned to, then it might cover up the drum and it won't cut through the mix.

"If there's a ring in the snare I might try to get it to ring in the key of the song, though, because sometimes that really sounds good."

Tuning the Snare Drum

Ross Garfield: "The snare is probably the most important drum in the set because it's the voice of the song since you hear it on at least every two and four, so it's important to get the snare tuned to where you want it first.

"If there are a few snare drums available, you should first try to pick the right snare drum for the song."

Snare Drum Tuning Tips

If the snare drum has too much ring:

- Tune the heads lower.
- Use a heavier head like a coated CS with the dot on the bottom or a coated Emperor.
- Use a full or partial muffling ring.
- Use an alternate snare drum.
- Have the edges checked and/or recut to a flatter angle.

If the snare drum doesn't have enough ring:

- Tune the head higher.
- Use a thinner head, like a coated Ambassador or Diplomat.
- Use an alternate snare drum.
- Have the edges checked and/or recut to a sharper angle.

If the snares buzz when the tom-toms are hit:

- Check that the snares are straight. Replace as needed.
- Check that the snares are flat and centered on the drum.
- Loosen the bottom head.
- Retune the offending toms.
- Use an alternate snare drum.

Tuning the Kick Drum

Ross Garfield: "I always find the kick drum to be pretty easy to tune because you tend to muffle it on almost every session and, when you do it, it makes tuning easier.

"What I would recommend is to take a down-filled pillow and set it so that it's sitting inside the drum, touching both heads (if it has a front head). If you want a deader sound then you push more pillow against the batter head, and if you want it livelier then you push it against the front head.

"Another way to go is to take a bath towel and fold it so it's touching both heads. If you need it deader, then put another one against both heads on top of the first one. If that's not enough then put another one in."

If the kick drum isn't punchy and lacks power when played in the context of the music, you can try the following:

- Try increasing and decreasing the amount of muffling in the drum, or try a different blanket or pillow.
- Change to a heavier, uncoated head, like a clear Emperor or PowerStroke 3.
- Change to a thinner front head or one with a larger cutout.
- Have the edges recut to create more attack.

Tuning the Toms

Ross Garfield: "The kick and snare are the two most important drums and I tune the toms around them to try to make sure that the rack toms aren't being set off by the snare.

"I like the toms to have a nice, even decay. Usually I'll tune the drums so that the smallest drums have the shortest decay, with the decay getting longer as the drums get bigger.

"I tend to tune each tom as far apart as the song will permit. It's easy to get the right spread between a 13" and a 16" tom, but it's more difficult to get it between a 12" and a 13". What I try to do is to tune the 12" up and the 13" down a little."

If one or more of the tom-toms are difficult to tune, don't blend together, or have an unwanted "growl," try the following:

- Check the top heads for dents and replace as necessary.
- Check the evenness of tension all around on the top and bottom heads.
- Tighten the bottom head.
- Have the bearing edges checked and recut, as required.

If the floor tom has an undesirable "basketball-type" after-ring, try this:

- Loosen the bottom head.
- Check the top heads for dents and replace as necessary.
- Loosen the top head.
- Switch to a different type or weight top or bottom head (like a clear Ambassador or Emperor). Have the bearing edges recut to emphasize the lower partials.

Cymbals

Ross Garfield: "For recording, you have to be careful when you mix cymbal weights. For example, if you're using thin Zildjian 'A Custom' crashes, you don't want to mix in a medium Rock Crash because a thinner cymbal would probably disappear in the mix.

"Thicker cymbals are made more with a live situation in mind. They're made to be loud and to cut through the band, but they can sound a little gong-like when recording. On the other hand, if you're playing all Rock Crashes and the engineer can deal with the level, that's not so bad either because the volume will be even.

"As far as cymbal suggestions for recording, I think the Paiste Signature heavy hi-hats record really well. I like the dry, heavy ride in a 20" or 21". I like the Power Ride in a 22" size. I like the Full Crashes in basically every size. I also really like the Zildjian 'A Custom' line from top to bottom and the K Custom hats in either 13", 14", or 15". The 22" K Custom ride in a heavy sounds good."

If the cymbals are cracking or breaking with greater frequency, try the following:

- Always transport the cymbals in a top-quality, reinforced cymbal case or bag to avoid nicks that can become cracks.
- Use the proper cymbals felts, washers, and sleeves at all times.
- Avoid over-tightening the cymbal stand.
- Use larger or heavier cymbals that you won't have to overplay to hear.

CHAPTER TWO

THE RECORDING ENVIRONMENT

You already know this but it's worth repeating. *The room in which you record has a lot to do with the sound of your drums.* You can have a great sounding kit that's tuned to perfection, but it won't sound nearly as good in a dead garage with an 8' ceiling as it will in well-designed studio with a 12' or 14' ceiling.

That being said, you can only work with what you have, so here are some tricks on how to optimize your room to make your kit sound its best in that acoustic environment.

ROOM RESONANT FREQUENCIES

Just about every room that hasn't been acoustically treated has a frequency that, when excited, is a lot more pronounced than others. What's more, this resonance will occur at even multiples of that frequency again and again.

Recording studio designers use many methods, including bass traps, absorbent surface treatment, and diffusers, to help eliminate these resonances. The problem is, if left untreated, these problematic bass frequencies can be responsible for the dreaded buzzing snare.

Small rooms with parallel walls tend to be much worse in this regard than those where the walls are slightly angled (like in most recording studios). If the bass, keyboard, or guitar player hit a note that's close to this troublesome frequency, the buzz will get worse because the volume of that note is accentuated and creates a sympathetic resonance within the drum.

While it's best to design and construct the room so these frequencies won't be a problem, that's not an option for most home studio owners. The next-best thing to do is to acoustically treat your room to keep those reflections to a minimum.

INEXPENSIVE YET EFFECTIVE ROOM TREATMENT

A frequently asked question by both drummers and engineers is: How do you make an environment originally designed for normal family use into one that's suitable for recording? If you feel like swinging a hammer a little and have a few dollars to spend, it's surprising how much you can actually improve the sound of a room.

That being said, you should know in advance that this process is broken down into two parts: soundproofing and acoustic treatment. Soundproofing is the process of isolating the room so the sound within doesn't leak out, and the sound of the outside world doesn't leak in. Acoustic treatment is the process of changing the acoustics of the room to eliminate unwanted reflections and low frequency buildup. If your recording room is very dead, you may actually want to liven it up a bit.

Soundproofing

One of the first questions that an engineer or drummer with a home studio asks is, "How can I make sure that my neighbors don't hear me?" There's really no secret to this one—all it takes is mass. Simply put, the more mass your room has (including cinder block, brick, wood, drywall, etc.), the more you'll be able to isolate the sound you make from the outside, as well as keep the sound of the outside world from getting in.

Most pro studios accomplish this by building a room within a room. This is done by putting the floor on springs or rubber isolators, and building double or triple walls with air spaces in between on top of the isolated floor. These air spaces between the walls act very much like shock absorbers.

Needless to say, this is really expensive and impossible to do if you start out with a small space (like a 10'x12' bedroom or garage) to begin with. There are other ways to increase the isolation that are quite a bit cheaper, although these may still not achieve the amount of soundproofing you need.

What Won't Work

Before we look at some accepted ways to improve your isolation, let's look at all the things that *won't* work. The following are various materials that you'll often see attached to the walls of a space in hopes of increasing the isolation.

- **Mattresses:** There are so many things wrong with this that it's hard to know where to start. Sure, mattresses are made up of a lot of soft material, but it's not the right kind for sound absorption; they won't affect the low frequencies at all (which are what cause most of the isolation problems); they accumulate mold and moisture; and they make nice homes for unwanted critters. Plus, it's pretty difficult to get enough of them to cover a room, and they take up an awful lot of space for so little benefit in return.
- **Egg Crates:** Egg crates are light porous cardboard that do absolutely nothing for soundproofing. They can act as a sound diffusor at higher frequencies, but the bandwidth is so limited that they're virtually useless there as well. Plus, they're highly flammable!
- **Carpet:** Carpet attached to the wall is another product that will affect the sound of the room yet do nothing in the way of soundproofing since it doesn't affect the low frequencies, which are the ones that you've got to control for good isolation. Carpet has exactly the same problem as mattresses in that it will begin to smell over time. Old or new carpet makes no difference, except that older carpet will smell worse.
- **Foam Rubber:** Foam rubber does have some acoustical absorption properties, but once again, will do very little for the low frequencies that will cause all of your problems with the neighbors. It can be as expensive as materials with real acoustic control properties, degrades over time, and will burn like crazy if given the chance.
- **Rubber:** Floor mats, mouse pads, neoprene, or any other variation of rubber will do very little to stop sound coming in or going out of your room. Once again, it's much cheaper to buy proper acoustic materials that are easier to work with, but they won't help your isolation problem, either.
- **Wall Cellulose:** Pumping cellulose insulation into walls can make a slight difference, but it's marginal since there are much more effective—and far cheaper—ways to improve the isolation. It can be helpful if used along with some other construction techniques, but isn't particularly effective by itself.
- **Fiberglass Insulation:** Common fiberglass insulation once again has little ability to stop enough of the low frequencies that bug your neighbors, although, like with blown cellulose, it can be useful in conjunction with other techniques. Just pinning it to

the wall won't help, though, but it *will* affect the acoustics of the room. It's also a skin and eye irritant, it takes up a lot of space, and the dust can be hazardous to your lungs when left exposed. As you'll soon see, there's a much better way to use fiberglass for acoustic control (although it still won't help much with isolation).

- **Plywood Panels:** It's true that plywood panels provide mass, and mass is what's needed to stop sound transmission (especially the low frequencies), but the problem is that wood transfers sound *too* well, so the construction technique used is crucial. Not only that, if the panels are too thin they'll resonate and vibrate, causing an even bigger problem.

- **Particle Board:** See plywood panels.

- **Bales of Hay:** Unless you live out in the country, it's unlikely that hay bales are much of an option, but they actually do work. The problem is that they take up a lot of usable space, make a nice home for rodents, and are a major fire hazard. Not recommended!

- **Acoustic Foam:** Acoustic foam is helpful in controlling the acoustics within a room, but it does *nothing* to stop sound transmission—and is expensive, to boot. Acoustic foam doesn't even begin to affect the offending low frequencies, and using too much just makes the room seem dead and uncomfortable. There are much cheaper ways to achieve a better result.

Understand that all of these materials will have at least some effect on the sound of the room, but will do almost nothing by themselves to help improve your isolation.

Improving the Isolation

Here are five steps to take to improve the isolation of just about any room. Keep in mind that we're talking an improvement and not total isolation. This improvement might meet your needs or it might not, depending upon many unpredictable variables. What might be enough for a playback area might not be enough to isolate a heavy-hitting drummer, for instance.

Step 1: Get the thickest solid core door that you can afford. A solid core door provides the maximum amount of isolation in a critical area that's often overlooked, but the trick is to make sure that there are no air spaces around the door. This is done by applying weather stripping around it on both sides so it closes with a tight seal. Test it by shining a flashlight around the closed door. If you can see the light at any point, then you have to reapply the weather stripping or the isolation will be compromised.

Step 2: Use a doorjamb. The doorjamb is often overlooked but it's extremely important to door isolation. A threshold affixed to the floor under the door provides a tight seal and maximizes the isolation, but makes it difficult to roll heavy amplifiers or equipment cases over it. That's why it's best to use a very low profile aluminum or wood floor threshold that has a rubber seal centered along the top (see Figure 2-1).

Figure 2-1: A studio door threshold.

There's also a type of door threshold that affixes to the bottom of the door and "drags" along the floor to create a seal. This works, but after a while it starts to wear down the floor or carpeting that it's dragging across, and sooner or later it's going to wear out. Whichever threshold you choose, it will take some initial adjusting, but you'll realize immediately that it was worth the effort once it's right.

Step 3: Treat the windows. Another source of sonic leakage can come from any windows that might be in the studio. While the best way to increase your isolation and eliminate any leakage is by totally plugging the window, the trend in studios these days is for lots of natural light. The easiest way to maintain some light and improve the isolation is to add a piece of half-inch Plexiglass to the outside of the window mounted on well-fitted weather stripping. If isolation is still a problem, the same can be done on the inside as well.

Step 4: Add some mass to the walls and ceiling. While you could add another sheet of drywall on top of the existing wall, the least expensive way to do this is with 3/8" cement backing board, which is the same thing used in showers (it's sometimes called "cement board"). It doesn't take up a lot of space and is more efficient than regular drywall. Cement board usually comes in 5'x3' panels, but they weigh about three times what a panel of 4'x8' drywall weighs. Make sure that the cement board is both glued and screwed since anything that isn't absolutely tight will either rattle or give the room an unwanted resonant ring later.

After the cement board is affixed to the wall, glue and screw some strips of quarter-inch low-grade, inexpensive industrial plywood to it, and then glue and screw half-inch regular drywall on top of that. The drywall is there primarily so there's an anchor to attach the wall treatment.

Step 5: Leave no air gaps. Leaks that allow the sound to violate the isolation is called "flanking transmission" and is a major cause of poor isolation. You can have four-foot- thick concrete walls but you can negate those benefits if there are air gaps anywhere in the room. This is especially true for doors, which are the greatest culprits for acoustic leakage, but can also be true of windows and seams between drywall. There can be no air gaps if you want maximum isolation. It's as simple as that.

It's best to use an acoustic sealant on these spaces because it doesn't break down with age, but any kind of caulking will work in a pinch. It's also important to have a tight seal around any light fixtures and on-off switches, AC outlets, mic panels, wall junctures, and HVAC vents.

If you follow these steps, you'll find that the isolation of your room will definitely increase, although it still might not be enough to contain the sound of a heavy-hitting drummer. True isolation relies on mass, which takes up space and is expensive to achieve.

Acoustic Treatment

While an in-depth look at room acoustics is beyond the scope of this book (check out *The Studio Builder's Handbook* for that), there are a few easy steps to take to control the acoustics of the room.

What does controlling the acoustics actually mean? Having a room that's reflective can be a good thing when recording drums, but those reflections have to be controlled. As stated before, reflections at the resonant frequency of the room can set off the drum's sympathetic vibrations and cause the snare to buzz. Fortunately, there are some easy ways to control this.

While many musicians resort to acoustic tiles like Sonex, they can be really expensive, especially if you need a lot of them. They're also not that effective in controlling low frequencies, which is where the real problems lie. Here are several other ways to accomplish the same thing for less money—and have it look better, too.

Option 1: Build or buy some acoustic panels. Acoustic panels are the major way that reflections are kept from bouncing around the room. You can think of an acoustic panel as a very large picture frame that has sound-absorbing material inside instead of a picture. Although you could permanently attach the sound-absorbing material to the wall (like most commercial studios do), using a sound panel allows you to move it as needed and even take it with you if you move.

Building an Acoustic Panel

Sound panels are very simple to make. They're based around an absorbent material like Owens Corning 703 rigid fiberglass board (the standard for acoustic treatment), or, to a lesser extent, Rockwool Rockboard 60. Either of these products come in standard 2'x4' panels in 1" to 6" thicknesses (2" is the most commonly used size). This differs from normal fiberglass batting in that it's a lot denser because it's tightly compressed, and although not made specifically for acoustic control, it works perfectly in this application.

The 703 is framed with simple 2"x2" or 2"x4" wood strip (see Figure 2-2), and then covered with a fabric-like burlap (the most popular) or Guilford of Maine, which is flame resistant but a lot more expensive (see Figure 2-3). The reason for using a 2"x4" frame instead of a 2"x2" (the size of the 703) is that the 2" air gap adds to the effectiveness of the panel by lowering the frequencies that it can absorb by an octave.

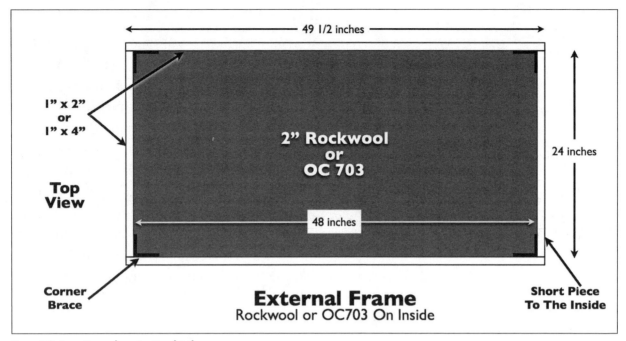

Figure 2-2: Acoustic panel construction details.

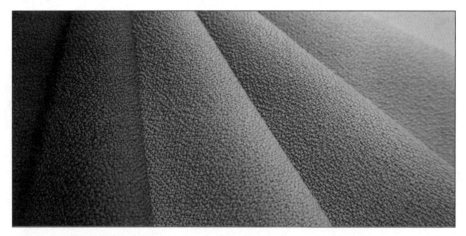

Figure 2-3: Guilford of Maine fabric.

Burlap works well as a cover because it won't sag and bag over time. The material is also cheap, it looks good, and is available in a very wide range of weaves and thicknesses. The general rule of thumb when selecting cloth is to breathe through it. If you can feel your breath on the other side, it's good to go, as sound can travel easily through it.

There are other products that are as effective for absorption as the 703. Owens Corning also makes a model 705 that has twice the density of the 703, but costs more as well. Speaking of cost, the 703 costs approximately $12 a panel (sometimes more and sometimes less, depending on where you buy it) and comes in packs of six. Knauf ECOSE, Johns Manville, Roxul Safe and Sound or Rockboard 60, and Certainteed all have the same absorption characteristics or better, and can be even less expensive than their Owens Corning equivalent.

You can see a video with detailed instructions on how to construct your own acoustic panels at youtube.com/user/polymedia.

Option 2: Purchase the acoustic panels. If you don't own a staple gun and have never swung a hammer, there's no need to worry. Numerous companies now sell their own versions of acoustic panels. Here's just a sampling:

atsacoustics.com
readyacoustics.com
gikacoustics.com
soundaway.com
acoustimac.com
realtraps.com
audimutesoundproofing.com
acousticalsolutions.com
perdueacoustics.com
msr-inc.com

If you choose to purchase acoustic panels from a company that isn't local, keep in mind that most panels are fairly large—2'x4'—so shipping charges may make them more expensive than you anticipated.

Option 3: Construct an acoustic panel alternative. There's yet another way to adjust the acoustics of the room that's built around half-inch carpet padding. It may not be traditional acoustic material, but it works and takes up a lot less room than acoustic tiles or panels. This works well at attenuating the high-frequency reflections of a room.

First buy a roll of half-inch carpet padding from your local home improvement or carpet store. Make a frame for the padding by using 1"x2" or 2"x2" plywood, and use the same wood to make runners down the middle.

Staple or nail the padding to the frame. You can then cover it with a fabric secured with staples (snug, but not too tight, or it will eventually ripple), then add some cosmetic wood strips to cover the staples. Your wall now looks great and there's some acoustic treatment in the room.

Treating the Floor

Most tracking rooms have reflective floors that are wood or cement, so there's no need to go overboard with treating the floor. All you need to do is put a light carpet under the drums to keep them from moving and also keep the reflections down.

That being said, the smaller the recording room becomes, the more you want to contain the ambience. That's because the reflections of a small room usually aren't that great sounding and we actually start to hear the smallness of the room, so the more you can keep them under control, the better the kit will sound.

Don't Forget the Air Conditioning

Now that your room is isolated and treated, you'll notice that it's pretty well insulated too. That means that it's going to get hot when even a few bodies get rocking inside (especially in the summer), so you'll have to consider some kind of air conditioning unit to keep everyone from falling over from heat exhaustion. Usually this is where things get really expensive in a professionally designed studio, since quietly exchanging the inside air with the outside takes a fair amount of expertise. Luckily there's a fairly inexpensive solution.

Check into the mini-split air conditioning systems that locate the compressor outside the building (see Figure 2-4). All that's required is a 1" hole cut through the wall to allow access for a hose to go to a cooling head, instead of the extensive ducting of an HVAC system. These systems are also available with a heat pump, which provides heating when the weather turns cold.

This cooling head is mounted on a wall and is very quiet. For a garage or a bedroom, a 9,000 BTU unit is normally enough to adequately cool or heat the space, and it's quiet enough that you can leave it on during drum recording and maybe even vocal recording as well. Make sure to clean the filter often to keep the noise down, and don't skimp on that yearly servicing.

Figure 2-4: Mini-split air conditioner.

The Curse of Low Ceilings

Low ceilings—those which are 8 feet tall or shorter—can be a problem for a couple reasons. First of all, the sound from the kit projects upwards and will splash off the ceiling (especially if it's a hard surface) back down towards the drums. This can result in frequency cancellation and alter the sound of the drums during recording.

Second, a low ceiling is the sworn enemy of overhead mics. This is because a low ceiling won't allow you to get the mics up high enough to capture enough of the kit without capturing some of those unwanted reflections, thereby altering the sound. A higher ceiling—measuring 12' to 15'—basically eliminates these problems.

There's not much you can do about changing the height of a ceiling, so the best thing is to relegate the overhead mics to close miking the cymbals. Another method is to affix a 2"x2'x2' foam acoustic pad just above the mic position to diminish the reflection coming back at the rear side of the mic, thus reducing phasing issues created by the low ceiling.

Optimizing Your Room Without Construction

If you're unable to make any physical changes to your room, there are still a few simple and easy things to do that will make a difference for the better. To tame the reflections in a live room, try taping up blankets, heavy cloth, or packing blankets to the walls (see Figures 2-5 and 2-6).

Figure 2-5: Changing the room acoustics using blankets.

Figure 2-6: Changing the room acoustics using cushions.

Tips and Tricks

For a more permanent solution to an overly live room, try half-inch (1.6 cm) thick by 6' (2 m) wide foam rubber carpet padding and attach it to the wall with a staple gun. Make sure you use staples that are long enough to hold the padding securely to the wall. A 10 yd (10m) roll costs about $20 (U.S. currency), and, with a few rolls, you can cover most rooms. This trick works so well that you want to be careful that you don't deaden the room *too* much. You can experiment and actually tune the room to get a personalized sound out of your recording area.

If the room is indeed too dead, try leaning some sheets of 3/8" (1 cm) plywood up against the wall. In a pinch, use some plastic sheeting or large plastic garbage bags opened flat and duct tape them to the walls. These create a reflective surface that should liven up your recording room.

PLACING THE KIT IN THE ROOM

If you do nothing else, positioning the kit in the best place in the room will do wonders for the sound. What you're looking for is a spot where the drums sound relatively live with a minimum of frequency cancellation from the room reflections.

A tip to remember: it's usually best to stay out of a corner. The corner will normally cause "bass loading," meaning that the low frequencies will be increased, causing the kick and floor tom to sound louder than the other drums. This can also lead to increased ringing and snare buzzing. That being said, sometimes more low end is just the thing you need, so don't rule the corner out without trying it first since the extra fullness of the kick might be just the thing you're looking for.

Pro engineers will usually test a room by walking around and clapping their hands, looking for a place that's has a nice, even reverb decay. If the clap has a *boing* to it (a funny overtone), then so will your drums, so it's best to try another place in the room.

Ideally, you don't want to be too close to a wall, either, since the reflections (or absorption, if the wall is soft) can also change the sound of the kit. The middle of the room usually works best.

You'll also want to utilize the place in the room where the ceiling is at its highest. If the ceiling is vaulted, try placing the drums in the middle of the vault first, and then move as needed.

Stay away from glass if you can, since it will give you the most unwanted reflections of just about any material. If you have no choice because of the way the room or the band must be situated, try setting up the kit at a 45° angle to the glass (see Figure 2-7).

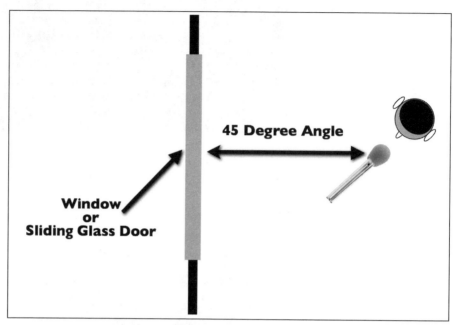

45 Degree Angle

Window or Sliding Glass Door

Figure 2-7: Setting up at an angle to the glass.

These tips will really help get your room in shape so you can get your drum sound off to the right start.

CHAPTER THREE

THE DRUMMER'S HEADPHONE MIX

A good headphone mix is probably the number one thing that makes a musician comfortable in the studio, and a comfortable musician will usually play a lot better than one who can't hear himself. Out of all the musicians recording, the drummer's needs are by far the most demanding.

Headphone Checklist:

✓ Headphones
✓ Headphone amp
✓ Headphone extension cable
✓ Duct tape

MICROPHONE CHOICE
Industry Standard: AKG K141 and 240, Sony 7506, Audio Technica M40 and M50, Fostex T-20
Popular Alternative: Isolation Headphones—Vic Firth S1H1 Headphones, Direct Sound EX-25 or EX-29
Inexpensive Substitute: Monoprice 8323

WHAT'S IN THE MIX?

The mix for the drummer is uniquely different from any of the other players due to the volume at which most drummers play. While all drummers have different preferences as to their cue mix, here's a good place to start.

1. **Make sure the kick is loud enough.** One reason for that is so that the drummer doesn't overhit it in order to hear himself. If you mix the kick (and the other drums for that matter) too loud in the headphones, though, you'll probably get a weak and uneven kick

drum performance. The drummer usually has no problem hearing his snare and toms acoustically, so they don't have to be as loud in the mix.

2. **Mix the bass and any percussion instruments louder as well.** It's important for the drummer to lock in with the bass player, so the bass level in the phones can be slightly louder than the other instruments.

3. **Tuck the other instruments and vocal just under the bass and kick.** The drummer usually uses the vocal just as a guide track to know where the various sections of the song begin.

4. **If you're using a click, it's usually the loudest thing in the mix.**

What you really want as a drummer is separate from what other people want. I think that there should be a rule that if there's a wall between you and another player, you need a different headphone mix.
—Bernie Dresel

If I'm tracking with a bass player and we're doing overdubs, I'll try to get a nice even level so it sounds like a record with the vocals and the bass player just above the music. I want to hear the bass player so I can be sure to lock my kick drum with him. Then if I'm tracking live I want whoever is the leader of the song to be above the track.
—Brian MacLeod

I like to hear the piano, a little bit of the bass, ambience on myself and whatever the lead instrument is so I can get a feel for the melody to know how to approach my particular part. Gotta have the click, too.
—Ricky Lawson

USING A CLICK TRACK

It'll be a debate that will last until the end of time regarding whether it's best to record with or without a click track, but most drummers today have at least some experience playing to one. There are a lot of advantages to using a click that really make it preferable, as long as the song doesn't come out sounding too stiff. For one thing, it makes editing between songs and sections easier, any time fixes to the track are easier, and it makes it a lot easier for the engineer to add time delays and reverb to the pulse of the song during the mix.

Many times just providing a click in the phones isn't enough. Here are some tricks to make the click not only listenable, but cut through the densest mixes and seem like another instrument in the track.

- **Pick the right sound.** Something that's more musical than an electronic click is better to groove to. Try a cowbell, a sidestick, or even a conga slap. Needless to say, when you pick a sound to replace the click, it should fit within the context of the song. Many drummers like two sounds for the click; something like a high go-go bell for the downbeat and a low go-go bell for the other beats, or vice-versa.
- **Make sure the downbeat is accented.** Most drummers might not care about the actual sound of the click as long as they have an accent on beat one.
- **Pick the right number of clicks per bar.** Some players like 1/4 notes while others play a lot better with 1/8ths. Whichever it is, it will work better if there's more emphasis on the downbeat (beat 1) than on the others.
- **Use an equalizer if needed.** Sometimes a little EQ at 3–4kHz can help the click cut through the mix. Be careful not to use too much, though, as it could cut so much that it will bleed into the microphones.
- **Make it groove.** Adding a little delay to the sound can make it swing a bit and not sound as stiff. This makes it easier for players who normally have trouble playing to a click. As a side benefit, this can help make any bleed that does occur less obvious, as it will seem like part of the song.

I begrudgingly use an electronic click, but I'd rather have a melodic one because they're really fun and easy to play to. If I had my choice I'd use a high go-go bell and a low go-go bell and then a side-stick for in-between [sings a rhythm], that way you always know where 1 and 3 and 2 and 4 are.

—Johnny "Vatos" Hernandez

I do not want a cowbell or a side-stick as a click. I don't want a musical sound because it affects what I think is happening musically. I want a non-musical sound that's really short.

—Bernie Dresel

Tips and Tricks

Always have the drummer record a count-off. It'll really come in handy during overdubs and you can just mute it later during the mix.

Preventing Click Bleed

Now that the click cuts through the mix, it might do it so well that it's now bleeding into the mics. If that's the case, try the following:

- **Change to a different headphone.** Try a pair that has a better seal. The Sony 7506 phones provide a fairly good seal, but a good pair of isolation headphones, like the Metrophones "Studio Kans" or the Vic Firth S1H1s (see Figure 3-1), will isolate a click from bleeding into nearby mics.

Figure 3-1: Vic Firth S1H1 isolation headphones.

- **Run the click through an equalizer** and roll off the high end just enough to cut down on the bleed.

A Click Alternative

If the drummer's performance with a click seems too stiff, try this method. It might help to provide not only the loosest feel but the best groove, too.

1. Record the song three times with the click.
2. Choose the best version.
3. Instead of a click, use the track for the drummer to play against by muting the drum part and just playing back the other instruments.
4. Proceed with recording overdubs.

Using the above method, the drummer can hear the rest of the band and play along through headphones so there should be very little bleed. Once the drums are printed, the session can progress as normal.

THE HEADPHONE SYSTEM

Headphone amplifiers used to be an area of concern in just about every studio, big or small, since for a long time there weren't any amps designed specifically for phones. In the early days of recording, the headphone amp consisted of a large power amp (the bigger the better) with some huge power resistors attached and a homemade headphone box. This jury-rigged system provided mixed results since the headphones didn't match up well with an amp that was designed to power a speaker.

These days many manufacturers make headphone amplifiers that are specifically designed for this one use. Companies like Behringer, Furman, PreSonus, Rolls, and Aphex all make units that will work better and can be a lot cheaper than the traditional method of a large power amp and resistors (see Figure 3-2).

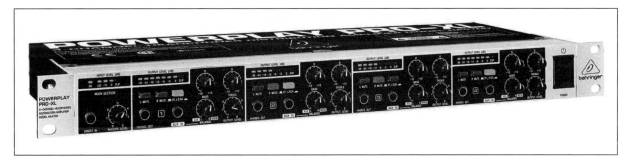

Figure 3-2: Behringer PowerPlay Pro-XL. *Courtesy of Behringer.*

Personal Headphone Mixes

Perhaps the best thing to come along in recent years has been the introduction of the relatively inexpensive "more me" personal headphone systems. These systems allow the musician to control his own headphone mix by supplying him with up to sixteen channels to control. Each headphone mixer/box also contains a headphone amplifier that can (depending upon the product) provide earsplitting levels. Manufacturers include Furman, Oz Audio, Aviom, and Hear Technologies (see Figure 3-3).

Figure 3-3: Hearback headphone system. *Courtesy of Hear Technologies.*

It's usually best to provide a stereo monitor mix (what you're listening to in the control room) to start with, as well as a separate track for kick, snare, vocal, and whatever other instruments are pertinent.

If you're not supplying a basic stereo mix, make sure to set the mix up for the drummer before recording begins. This is important because many musicians like to have the flexibility of the separate mix but just can't seem to come up with an adequate one when left to their own devices. It's best if you set the mix up beforehand, then walk the drummer through each of the controls so he can then adjust the mix as needed.

CHAPTER FOUR
PHASE CANCELLATION— THE DRUM SOUND DESTROYER

Throughout this book we'll constantly be referring to phase cancellation, and with good reason.

One of the most important and overlooked aspects of drum miking is making sure that the mics are all in-phase. This is really important because with only one out-of-phase mic, the whole kit will never sound right, and if not corrected before all the drums are mixed together, can never be fixed.

So, just what is phase anyway? Without getting into a heavy explanation, it just means that all the microphones are pushing and pulling together (see Figure 4-1). If one mic is pushing while another is pulling, some frequencies cancel each other out (see Figure 4-2).

In this figure, both mics are pushing and pulling together. Their signal peaks happen at the same time as do their valleys. As a result, their signals reinforce one another.

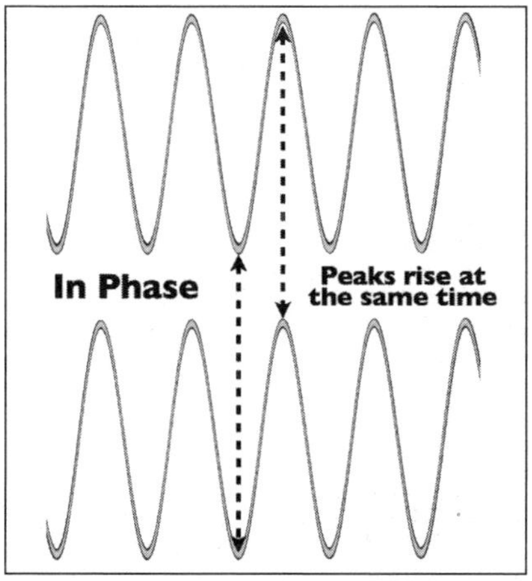

In Figure 4-2, when mic 1's signal peaks, mic 2's signal valleys. They cancel each other out and result in a very weak sounding signal when mixed together.

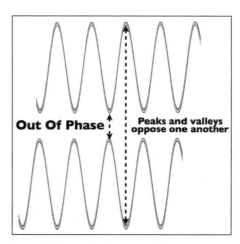

Figure 4-1: Two microphones in-phase.

Figure 4-2: Two microphones out-of-phase.

ACOUSTIC PHASE CANCELLATION

There are two types of phasing problems that can happen—electronic and acoustic. An acoustic phasing problem occurs when two mics are close together and pick up the same signal at the same time, only one is picking it up a little later than the first because it's a little farther away (see Figure 4-3).

Figure 4-3: Acoustically out of phase.

When acoustic phase problems occur, the audio from each mic won't cancel each other out completely, only at certain frequencies. This usually makes the audio from the two mics mixed together sound either hollow or just lack depth and bottom end.

The way to eliminate the problem is by moving mic 2 to a distance that's three times the distance that mic 1 is to the source. For example, if mic 1 is a foot away from the source, mic 2 should be around three feet from the same source to eliminate any acoustic phase problems (see Figure 4-4). This is called the "3 to 1 rule."

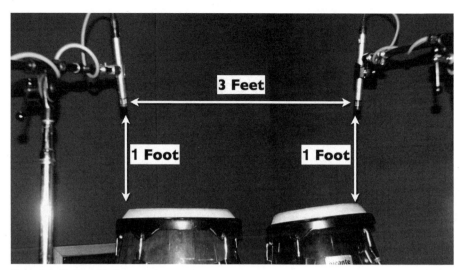

Figure 4-4: The 3 to 1 Rule.

The 3 to 1 rule doesn't have to be strictly observed in that you don't need to get out your tape measure every time you place your drum mics. Just keep in mind that if you have enough distance between the mics then you should be alright in most situations.

Another way to adjust for acoustic phasing problems takes into consideration the directionality of the mics. If you're using directional mics (which will probably be the majority of the time), make sure that each one is pointing directly at the source that they're trying to capture, like you'll see in chapter eight on tom miking (see Figure 8-5). Keeping the mics parallel to each other, or at a 45° angle for mics underneath drums will also really make a difference.

ELECTRONIC PHASE CANCELLATION

All the way through this book you'll see different examples of how to avoid acoustic phase problems, but electronic phasing of the mics is just as important.

Why would there be an electronic phase problem? Most of the time it's because a mic cable was mis-wired (either repaired incorrectly or originally wired incorrectly from the factory), or the microphone itself is sending a signal that's out-of-phase from the other mics you're using. In other words, one mic is outputing a positive voltage on pin 2 of the XLR connector when the other mics are outputing negative on pin 3. This is something that was more prevalent in the days before XLR connections were standardized, so it's not much of a problem now unless you're using a vintage mic.

Regardless of how it happens, there are two ways to check the electronic phase.

Checking Phase the Easy Way

There's a very easy way to check mic phase. After you get a mix balance of the kit together, flip the phase selector on each mic channel one at a time, either on your console or in the DAW. Whichever position has the most low end, leave it there. Do this on every mic in the kit (select the overhead and room mics in a pair, but check the left mic against the right as well).

Checking Phase the Slightly More Difficult Way

This method takes a bit more work, but you'll know for sure if you have a mic cable that's wired backward. Also, you really have to have another person with you to make this work. It's a two-man operation.

First, you have to pick a mic and make it your "reference." Any mic on the kit will do, but it's easier to pick a mic that can easily come off the stand.

Now take your reference mic and put it next to another mic on the kit, say the kick drum mic, as in Figure 4-5. Make sure that each mic is at the exact same volume level (this is important!). Now have someone talk into the mic while you switch the phase selector on either the console or DAW. Again, choose the selection that sounds the fullest.

Do this to each microphone. Any channel that has its phase selector different from all the others has a mis-wired cable. Make sure you mark it so you don't have the same problem again!

Figure 4-5: Checking the electronic phase.

TIMES WHEN YOU MIGHT WANT THE PHASE REVERSED

There are times when you should definitely consider flipping the phase on a drum mic because it's placed farther away than another mic yet it's picking up the same source. In the following cases, try engaging the phase button and select the position that provides the most low end.

- **An Under-Snare Mic:** As we'll discuss in chapter six, the under-snare mic should just about always be flipped out-of-phase.
- **Room Mics:** Depending on where they're placed, how much room reflection they're receiving, and the level that they're used in the mix, sometimes the room mics sound a lot better if the phase is reversed.
- **Overhead Mics in Extremely Rare Cases:** Once again, it depends on how high they're placed above the kit, the kind of reflections they're receiving, and if they're the main sound of the kit. On rare occasions it might sound fuller if the phase is flipped.

Tips and Tricks

Try checking phase in mono on a single speaker. t will be a lot easier to hear any differences.

CHAPTER FIVE

MIKING THE BASS DRUM

any engineers obsess over the kick drum sound, and well they should. The kick provides the pulse of the song as well as being part of the foundation of the rhythm section. A wimpy-sounding kick will usually result in a wimpy-sounding recording and something that's extremely difficult to save in the mix, so it's usually best to spend whatever time's necessary to make it sound great before recording.

Bass Drum Checklist:

✓ Large diaphragm dynamic mic with cable
✓ Short mic boom stand
✓ Rug or carpet
✓ Packing blanket, pillow, or cushion
✓ Brick, sandbag, or heavy weight (optional)

MICROPHONE CHOICE

Industry Standard: The Shure Beta 52 sounds very consistent over different dynamic levels. Some mics will change their tone (usually becoming brighter in the midrange) at very loud levels. If a Beta 52 is not available, try any large diaphragm mic that's available.

Popular Alternative: Sennheiser 421, Audix D6, AKG D112, E/V RE20, Shure Beta 91, U47-FET

Inexpensive Substitute: AKG D112, Shure SM58 if it's the only thing available (try adding a couple of dB at 60 or 100Hz and pull out a couple at 1.5kHz to make it work).

CHOOSING THE MIC

Most engineers start getting their drums sounds with the bass or kick drum, since it often takes more time to get it recording ready than the rest of the kit.

For miking the bass drum, the most common choice is to use a large diaphragm dynamic mic, although a high-end large diaphragm condenser mic can also work well and produce a big, punchy sound.

Be aware that if you use a condenser mic (especially an inexpensive one), there's the risk of overloading its diaphragm or internal preamp with a heavy-hitting drummer. This can result in what sounds like a blown speaker, so it might not be a good alternative for every situation.

Don't be afraid to experiment with other choices, however, since every song, arrangement, kick drum, and drummer are unique. What works on one song may not work on another, and vice versa.

Also remember that you can sometimes be fooled by the sound of kick played by itself. What sounded big and wonderful in the room during sound check may not work in the track once the other instruments begin playing, so be prepared to try a different mic position, different mic, even a different kick drum.

BASS DRUM HEAD CONFIGURATION

For most—but not all—applications, the best sound comes from a bass drum with only one head. There are exceptions to this, depending upon the genre of music, since that kind of sound might be out of place in a jazz or classical piece.

Front Head Removed

Removing the front bass drum head (the one facing the audience) usually results in a tighter and more direct sound. That said, the feel of the bass drum is different with the front head on, and this configuration might be more comfortable to the drummer if that's the way he's used to playing. It does affect the sound, since both heads resonate differently, causing some phase cancellation to occur within the drum itself, which may be just the sound you're looking for (it worked well for John Bonham, after all).

As a compromise, many drummers will cut a hole in the front head. This could work well for recording, but it also might cause some unwanted overtones, which could make the bass drum sound cloudy and muffled. One way to control this is to lean a packing blanket against the front head (see Figure 5-1), although a better way is to remove the front head and place a pillow, towel, or blanket inside the drum so it touches both heads once the front head is replaced.

Figure 5-1: Using a packing blanket to muffle the overtones.

Front Head On

If the drummer prefers to have the front head remain on the bass drum and doesn't want to cut a hole in it, you may also want to use some padding and duct tape to mute any unwanted overtones.

To preview the bass drum with and without overtones, place your hand on the front head to deaden it, while someone kicks the pedal, and listen to the difference. If you like what you hear when your hand is on the head, tape some padding where your hand was. If you're looking for a sound that's more like when your hand is off the head, then leave the front head bare.

BASS DRUM MIC POSITIONING

Where the mic is positioned when miking the kick drum provides a wide range of different sounds. If the drummer has taken the front head off, place the mic on a short boom stand, place the stand on the floor in front of the bass drum, and position the head element of the mic just inside the drum by a couple of inches.

Without the Front Head

Try pointing the front of the mic toward the center of the bass drum beater head, about 8"–12" (25–38 cm) away from the inside head, at about the same height as where the beater hits the drum (see Figure 5-2).

Figure 5-2: Starting mic position for bass drum with no front head.

To get a tighter, more compact bass drum sound, place a folded packing blanket or a pillow on the inside of the bottom of the drum shell, lightly touching the head (see Figure 5-3). Secure it with a weight (even a brick will do) to keep the blanket or pillow from slipping once you've positioned it to get the desired sound.

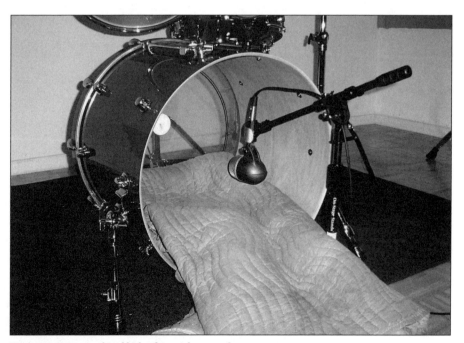

Figure 5-3: Using a packing blanket for a tighter sound.

With the Front Head

If you're miking a bass drum with a front head, try putting the mic on a short stand about 4" (13 cm) away from the head, halfway up and off-center (see Figure 5-4).

Figure 5-4: Miking a bass drum with a front head.

If you're miking a drum with a front head that has a hole, place the mic just inside the hole and pointed at the spot where the beater strikes the back head (see Figure 5-5).

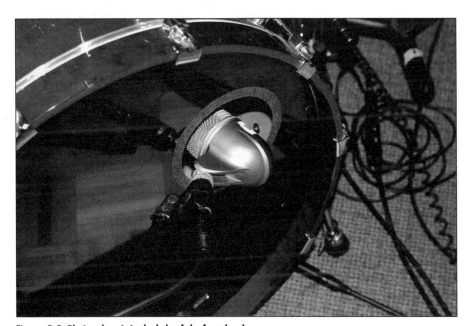

Figure 5-5: Placing the mic in the hole of the front head.

Increasing the Isolation

Sometimes the bass drum mic requires more isolation since it might be picking up too much of the rest of the kit. This is especially true when you're miking the bass drum with a front head since the mic is placed back in the room a bit.

The way around this is to cover the mic and the front of the bass drum with a heavy packing blanket (see Figure 5-6). This will increase the isolation, but it may change the sound a bit as well. Use some gaffers tape (which doesn't leave any residue) to keep the blanket from shaking loose while the drummer is playing.

Figure 5-6: Using a blanket for increased isolation.

Increasing the Low End

If you don't have a sub-kick setup, there is another way to increase the low end by adding a second mic about 6 feet back from the edge of the outside rim of the drum. This will usually pick up a lot more low end, but it will also pick up every other drum and cymbal in the kit, as well as other instruments being played. The way to get some additional isolation is to build a "kick drum tunnel," which is simply a couple of packing blankets draped around a few chairs that extends from the kick drum to the "out" microphone (see Figure 5-7).

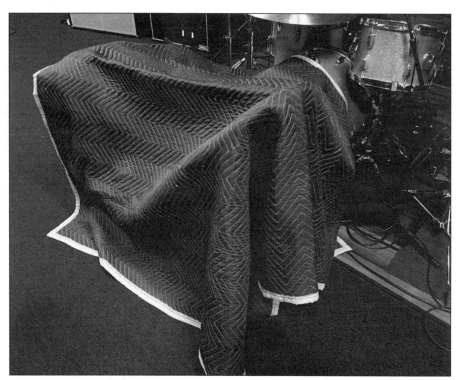

Figure 5-7: A kick drum tunnel.

BASS DRUM SOUND CHECK

After the mic has been positioned and the kick sounds great acoustically, the next step is to set the recording level and adjust the equalization on the bass drum. At this point, have the drummer do a steady slow beat on the bass drum only, at about one beat per second. This provides enough time to adequately hear the decay of the drum (which contains most of the tone).

If a sharper attack on the bass drum is needed, try adding a bit at 5kHz. For a larger, boomier bass drum, add a bit at somewhere between 50Hz to 100Hz. If you select a frequency too much above 100Hz, the kick will begin to sound "muffy" or "boxy."

Sometimes it makes sense to attenuate the mid-range frequencies at about 1.5kHz to get out the "thickness" or duck quack sound of the kick drum (especially if you're using a small diaphragm dynamic mic like a 421 or SM57). Some engineers cut somewhere in the 160Hz to 400Hz range to get rid of a kick's "beach ball" sound as well.

Experiment with your sound before you commit to a final decision. If you try moving the mic away from the head in 1" (3 cm) increments, you may be able to capture a fuller sound.

ADDING COMPRESSION

If the drummer has a hitting technique in which the kick varies in level from hit to hit, you can even it out somewhat by using a bit of compression. Most professional session drummers don't have this problem, but even for the pros a bit of compression might change the tonal balance of the kick for the better as it will make it more "punchy" sounding.

When using a compressor during recording, add it sparingly with a 2:1 ratio and no more than 1 or 2dB of gain reduction with a very fast release, and a quick 3–7 ms attack. If the release time is too slow, you may hear the signal pumping, where it goes from quiet to loud as the limiter releases. If the compressor has an "over-easy" mode where it causes the unit to go smoothly from no compression to compression, try that as well, but be aware that it might affect the high-end frequency balance.

Before adding any compression, listen to the drummer hit the bass drum without the compression first, then compare it to the sound with compression. Remember, as with any effect, once it's recorded into the audio file, it's there for good. If you're not totally satisfied with the sound, or you're unsure as to the amount of compression, it's always possible to add compression during the mixing stage.

THE SUB-KICK

The sub-kick phenomenon started pretty recently due to the burning desire to get more bottom end out of the kick drum without having to crank up the EQ. It's actually a small speaker (anywhere from 5"–6 1/2") that's been rewired to be used as a microphone to pick up the ultra-lows of a kick drum below about 50Hz that most mics just can't capture. While a sub-kick can be jury-rigged by taking the low-frequency driver from a small monitor, Yamaha also makes a commercial version known as the SKRM-100 (see Figure 5-8).

While this might sound like a new idea, it's hardly new. In fact, engineer Geoff Emerick used a speaker cabinet as a microphone way

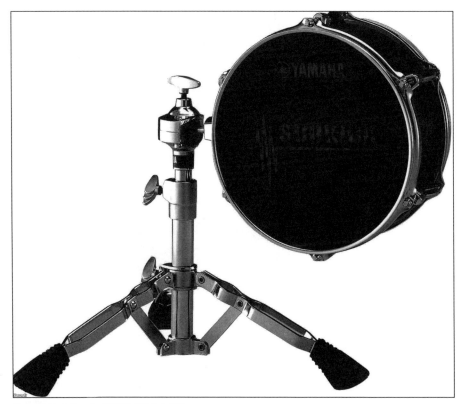

Figure 5-8: A Yamaha SKRM 100 Sub-kick.

back in 1966 on The Beatles' "Paperback Writer." Since then, count-less studios have employed their own versions of the same trick.

The first time I saw the technique was back when I was working for Mo-town in the mid-'70s. Sy Mitchell, one of Motown's frequent tracking engineers, wanted to get a hi-hat track that was totally isolated, so he had one of the guys in the maintenance shop (every large studio had one back then) wire up a microphone out of a Sennheiser headphone element. He taped it on the hi-hat about an inch from the bell so it went up and down with the hat. Although it didn't sound that great, it did work incredibly well. The hat was totally isolated from the snare.
—Dennis Moody

Making a Sub-kick Mic

Making a sub-kick mic is fairly easy. Just wire pins 2 and 3 of an XLR connector to the terminals of a small speaker (see Figure 5-9). The only thing to be aware of is that the phase could be backward, so you might have to rewire the XLR so it connects to the opposite terminals. It became popular to take the woofer from a Yamaha NS-10M and

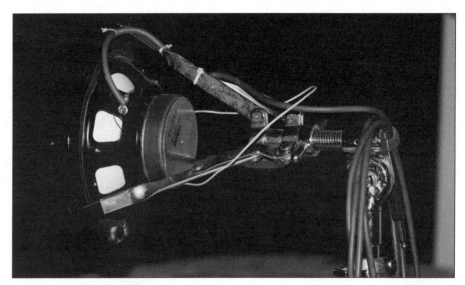

Figure 5-9: A home-made sub-kick.

use the magnet to attach it to a mic stand about 2" in front of the bass drum. The problem is, Yamaha no longer produces the NS-10, and the factory that made the woofer has been closed. Yamaha's SKRM-1000 has a 10" speaker mounted inside a 7-ply maple drum shell with black mesh heads, so it's actually a speaker mounted inside a 10" drum. DW also makes a version called the Moon Mic (see Figure 5-10).

Figure 5-10: A DW Moon mic.

Although the Yamaha sub-kick can be tuned, many engineers don't like the sound as much as the homemade version made from the raw NS-10 woofer. The factory version emphasizes the frequencies about an octave higher than what comes from an official NS-10 woofer.

Tips and Tricks

Get the kick drum sounding great first, then add only about 10 percent of that level of the sub-kick to the kick sound, then back it off a little. Be aware that if your speakers won't reproduce 50Hz and below, then you won't hear much of the sub-kick, which can cause you to add too much in the mix, resulting in a rather "boomy" sound.

The sub-kick can be used on other instruments as well. Try it on a bass amp, or even a trombone.

CHAPTER SIX

MIKING THE SNARE DRUM

The snare drum is the pulse of the song and therefore the most important drum in the kit. Many engineers struggle to get the right sound for the track, but so much of it has to do with the sound of the entire kit, not the snare by itself. That said, there are a number of ways to capture a great snare sound.

Snare Drum Equipment Checklist:

✓ Medium mic boom stand
✓ Compressor (optional)
✓ Inline phase reversal barrel (optional)

MICROPHONE CHOICE
Industry Standard: Shure SM57, Beta 57a
Popular Alternative: Neumann KM84, AKG451, Shure Beta 87a
Inexpensive Substitute: Audix i5

The SM57 is the de facto standard for miking the snare, mostly because it's able to take the super-loud level of a snare hit without overloading or changing its frequency response. That said, many times the 57 doesn't always deliver the high end that many engineers, drummers and producers are looking for.

In order to capture more of the actual snare sound without having to resort to high-end EQ later, some engineers prefer the sound of a small diaphragm condenser mic like a Neumann KM84 or AKG451, but it's important that these be used with attenuation pads in order to keep the mic preamp from overloading due to the high level the mic sees at the snare head.

Some engineers like the sound of a 57 and a small diaphragm condenser mic together, but setting up two stands and then positioning both mics close enough so there's no phasing issues isn't very easy. As a result, many have resorted to taping the two mics together, which can be messy when cleaning up after the session. If this is something that you want to try, the X Clip is an ingenious way of mounting both microphones together with the least amount of hassle (see Figure 6-1).

Figure 6-1: The X Clip dual microphone clip.

Many engineers now prefer the new Shure Beta 57a on snare because of its tight pickup pattern, extended frequency response, and higher output. It can be noticeably better in rejecting leakage from the hi-hat than a normal 57.

SNARE MIC POSITION
Place the mic on a boom stand and position it in front of the snare, until it rests about 1" (3 cm), or about 2 of your fingers, above the rim and in toward the center of the drum to where the mic head meets the body with a silver ring of the SM57 (if that's the mic you're using). Make sure there's a slight angle so the mic is pointed towards the center of the drum head (see Figure 6-2). Also make sure that the mic stand isn't touching any drum hardware to prevent the mic from picking up any unwanted vibrations.

In order to get some isolation from the other drums and cymbals, it's best if the snare mic is pointing away from the hi-hats, which can get tricky as sometimes that position gets in the way of the drummer. That's not something you want, as you may wind up recording some random stick hits, and maybe even have the mic damaged in the process. A good place is directly between the rack tom and hi-hats, if it's out of the way of the drummer.

Figure 6-2: Mic position for the snare drum.

SNARE MIC SOUND CHECK

To get a working level, have the drummer hit the snare at about one hit per second to check the tone. After the level has been adjusted, have the drummer play the song at full volume and see if the tone has changed.

Keep in mind that regardless of how the snare sounds by itself, its tone will change as soon as the other drum mics are added. That's why it's always a good idea to approach the drums as a single instrument rather than a collection of miked drums.

Unlike the bass drum, you'll rarely need to move the snare mic from this position to find a particular sound. Because the snare drum is so incredibly loud and the mic is placed only a few inches away, a mic other than a 57 that works perfectly well at low volumes may not sound the same when trying to capture a heavy drum beat.

To make the sound a bit more crisp, add some EQ at 10–12kHz. To add some "point," add at 3,500Hz to 5kHz. To make it fatter, add at 80–110Hz.

SNARE DRUM BOTTOM HEAD MIKING

In order to capture more of the sound of the snare strainers, many engineers add a second mic under the snare. This captures some of the crispness of the drum that the top mic won't hear. When added to the main, top snare mic, it provides the nice high-end snap without having to resort to much EQ.

There are several different theories on what mic to use for this purpose. Some engineers don't feel the quality of this mic is that important, since it's only meant to capture some of the high-frequency snap of the drum. As a result, they feel that any extra mic lying around the studio will do.

Other engineers wanting a fuller sound are more particular about how the bottom mic sounds. In that case, the directionality of the mic is most important so it doesn't pick up as much of the bass drum. In this case, the ultra-directional Sennheiser MD-441 is a perfect but expensive fit, while the much cheaper Shure Beta87a works as well.

Regardless of your choice for a bottom snare mic, the key is to place it as close to a 90° angle to the top snare mic as you can. This will control the phase cancellation and give you some additional rejection from the other drums and cymbals. Also remember to insert a pad on the mic and select any low-frequency roll-off that's available to keep out as much of the bass drum as possible (see Figure 6-3).

If you do mike the bottom head, make sure you check the phase between the bottom and top snare mics. Listen to the snare while the drummer is hitting it and select the phase button on your console, preamp, or DAW. Choose the position that gives you the fullest sound. Perhaps 90 percent of the time you'll have to reverse the phase on the bottom mic.

In some rare cases a phase switch isn't available on your console or preamp. A way around this is to purchase a phase-reversal "barrel" at your local music or electronic store. They usually run about $15 (U.S. currency) (see Figure 6-4).

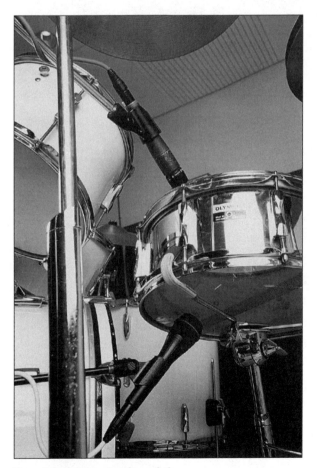

Figure 6-3: Placing a mic underneath the snare.

Figure 6-4: In-line phase reversal barrel.

For more detailed tips and tricks on phase and phase correction, check out *The Recording Engineer's Handbook* and *The Mixing Engineer's Handbook*.

The Bottom Mic in the Mix

Be careful how much of the bottom mic you add to the mix, because if you add too much the snare will start to sound thin and paper-like. A good rule of thumb is to add it to the point where you can just hear it in the mix, and then back it off a little.

If you're still learning how to record drums, it's a good idea to use only a top mic to get started. After you feel confident with positioning the top mic (and the sound it captures), try adding a bottom mic to see if you like what it adds to the snare sound.

Getting a good, balanced sound from the bottom head of a snare can be tricky, so don't get discouraged if it takes several tries to get it right. Make sure to keep the top and bottom snare mics recorded on two separate channels so you have more control later when you mix.

Also, the deeper the snare drum, the more effective it will be when adding the bottom snare mic. If you're using a 4"–5"-deep snare, adding the bottom mic will be less effective than when recording an 8"–10+"-deep snare drum.

ADDING COMPRESSION TO THE SNARE SOUND

As with the kick drum, compression on the snare can make it sound more aggressive or compensate for uneven hits from the drummer. Remember that if you add it when recording, the effect will then be married to the track and can't be adjusted later. If you compress it too much, the natural sound of the drum might start sounding like an artificial snare sample because you're reducing or eliminating its natural dynamics.

A good rule of thumb while recording is to use about a 2:1 ratio setting with fast attack and release, and only compress it by about 1 dB or so, just to smooth out the peaks.

Of course, if you want something that's very aggressive and unnatural sounding, then crank up the compression, although this might be better left for the mix. Be careful, though, since too much will result in all the life and attack being squeezed out of the sound.

Using a compressor on a snare will also allow you to more easily hear all the little grace notes the drummer is playing. Be careful not to over-compress in order to make these grace notes more audible.

CHAPTER SEVEN
MIKING THE HI-HAT

The hi-hat is the rhythm of kit, providing not only movement to the song but also some high-end sparkle to the kit. Because the hat can spill over into the other drum mics, some engineers don't even choose to mike it. If you really want some control over the final drum sound in the mix, however, it's something you'll always do without thinking.

Hi-Hat Equipment Checklist:

✓ Small diaphragm condenser mic
✓ -10dB pad (if not available on your mic pre or console preamp)
✓ Medium mic boom stand

MICROPHONE CHOICE
Industry Standard: Neumann KM84 or 184, AKG 451
Popular Alternative: Shure SM81, AT4051, Shure KSM137 or 141, Shure SM7B
Inexpensive Substitute: MXL 2003, Rode NT3

While the kick and snare seem to have particular favorite microphones that you'll see used over and over again, engineers have a somewhat wider palette for hi-hat mics. Even though there's no single standard mic, there is a type of mic that's frequently used. These are the small diaphragm condenser mics like a Neumann KM84 or 184, AKG 451 or 460, or Shure SM81.

Small diaphragm condenser mics work well in this situation because they have the quick, transient response needed to accurately capture the sharp attack of the hat. Of course, all mics in this category are not created equally, and some perform better than others, which means a more natural sound.

Another microphone parameter worth considering is the pickup pattern. The more directional the pattern, the less leakage will be captured from the rest of the drum kit. A hyper-cardioid pickup pattern is preferred, but, usually, a plain cardioid is what will be available.

Regardless of which mic you choose, if it is a condenser mic, be sure to use a -10dB attenuator pad to prevent any overloads to the mic's internal preamp or the microphone preamp that it's connected to. On most of the condenser mics you'll be using for the hi-hats, the switch to implement the pad will be on the side of the microphone and may be marked -10dB, -15dB or -20dB (see Figure 7-1).

Figure 7-1: Microphone low-frequency roll-off and attenuator pad.

If your mic doesn't have this, you can purchase a -10dB in-line attenuator barrel from your local music or electronic supply store (see Figure 7-2).

Figure 7-2: An in-line attenuator pad.

HI-HAT MIC POSITIONING

First, make sure that the mic is placed towards the rear of the kit as far away from the crash cymbal, if possible.

Place the mic about halfway between the bell and the edge of the top cymbal, pointing directly down. Position the mic up about 6 inches (20 cm) over the top cymbal when it's open, since this position picks up more of the overall tone of the cymbals (see Figure 7-3).

Figure 7-3: Hi-hat mic placement.

Remember to place the hi-hat mic as close to a 45° angle to the snare mic as possible, as this will help decrease any potential phase problems. Be careful not to move the mic too close to the hat as this will capture a sound that may be too thick for the mix. To make the sound thinner, move the mic out towards the edge a bit more, but away from the snare drum (see Figure 7-4).

Figure 7-4: Mic placement for a thinner hat sound.

You might think that placing a mic right on the edge looking in at the hat might be a good idea, but this doesn't work because of the massive puff of air that emanates when the hat closes. It sounds good in theory but doesn't work in reality (see Figure 7-5).

Figure 7-5: Don't mike the hi-hats this way.

If the drummer has a really huge set, sometimes there's just no room to mike the hat from the top. In this rare case, you might consider miking it from the bottom. As with the other instances where a mic is used underneath a drum or cymbal, place it at a 45° angle to the snare mic, and experiment with flipping the phase switch to get the fullest sound.

HI-HAT MIC SOUND CHECK

Once again, have the drummer play the hi-hat and listen to the sound. Before you apply any EQ, move the mic either closer to the top hat or farther away to make the sound thicker or thinner. Also try moving the mic closer to the edge of the cymbal for the thinner sound, or closer to the bell to make it thicker. You can also decrease the 1.2kHz range by 2 or 3dB to thin the hats out.

If the hat still needs some sizzle, add a few dB at 10 or 12kHz. Also, you might want to filter out anything below 140kHz, using the high-pass filter on the console or preamp, as this will decrease the low frequency leakage from the rest of the kit, especially the kick drum. Of course, an easy way to alter the sound if it's too thick is to try thinner and smaller hi-hats.

> ### Tips and Tricks
>
> When I was working with Motown Records in the late '70s, I picked up quite a cool little hi-hat recording trick. If you're after that old mid-1970s Motown "disco hi-hat" sound, mike the top cymbal by pointing directly at the bell of the top cymbal, about 1" (3 cm) away in the open position (see Figure 7-6). We used to use an E/V RE-15 microphone, but I've found this works well with any dynamic mic. Start with this positioning, experiment with the EQ, and blame it on the boogie.
>
> —Dennis Moody

Figure 7-6: Mic placement for '70s Motown sound.

CHAPTER EIGHT
MIKING THE TOMS

While the kick and snare are integral to the sound of the song, it's usually the toms that actually define a drum kit's sound. Great sounding toms just scream great sounding kit, so capturing them at their best is an engineer's top priority.

Tom Equipment Checklist:

✓ Condenser or dynamic mics
✓ Medium mic boom stands
✓ Clip-on or rim-mounted drum microphones

MICROPHONE CHOICE
Industry Standard: Sennheiser MD-421, AKG 414
Popular Alternative: Shure SM57, Neumann U87, Shure Beta 98/S, Shure KSM44, AT4040 or 4050, Audix D4
Inexpensive Substitute: Studio Projects B1

The toms require a mic that sounds full and is at the same time directional enough to decrease the leakage from the other drums and cymbals. While many engineers opt for the Sennheiser 421, others find the midrange of the mic to be too harsh and prefer a large diaphragm condenser mic like the Neumann U87, AKG 451, AKG 414 or AT4040 or 4050. Condenser mics are better able to capture the transients of the instrument than dynamic mics. As a result, you'll hear more of the attack of the drum and less of a thump when using a condenser mic rather than a dynamic.

One of the main attributes of a mic like the Shure SM98/S is that it's very small and attaches directly to the drum, which eliminates the need for mic stands and makes it easier to keep out of the way of cymbals and sticks. When using a clip-on mic, make sure that it's mounted tightly because it might loosen from the vibration and fall off during a song. Check with the drummer before you mount anything on his kit, though, as some drummers are very sensitive about having things attached to their kit. Also, make sure that the rim-mounted mic is not constricting the sound of the drum.

Because of the high sound pressure level that comes at the instant the tom is struck by the stick, when using a condenser mic it's best to switch on the -10dB pad, if the mic has one. Because condenser mics are more sensitive than dynamic microphones, you may have to move it away from the head a little more (see Figure 8-3) to keep it from distorting as well. This will also increase the leakage from the rest of the kit, but that might be just the sound you're looking for (a jazz date comes to mind).

As with the other components of the drum kit, make sure the toms sound great acoustically before placing a mic. If necessary, use a little masking tape or Moongel (see Figure 8-1) to take out any excessive ringing, but remember that the ring is part of the sound, too.

If you decide that you need to tame a ring, try using a small amount (1"x3") of console masking tape or gaffers tape to dampen a ring without appreciably decreasing the snap of the drum. Tape it about 3/4 of an inch from the edge of the batter head, pull it back a bit, and then stick it down over the hoop on the outside of the drum. Done correctly, it should stick onto the batter head for only about half of the tape's length. "Deadringers," which are half-inch-wide rings of thin plastic that go over the periphery of the batter head, do a similar job but can eat up too much of the drum's tone.

As with all padding, use it sparingly and don't deaden the sound too much, unless that's the effect you're looking for.

Figure 8-1: MoonGel damper pads.

RACK TOM MIC POSITIONING

The classic tom miking method is to place the mic two to three inches off the head above the rim (about three fingers above the edge) at a 45° angle, looking down at the center of the head to get the most attack (see Figure 8-2). For more ring and less attack, point the mic closer to the rim.

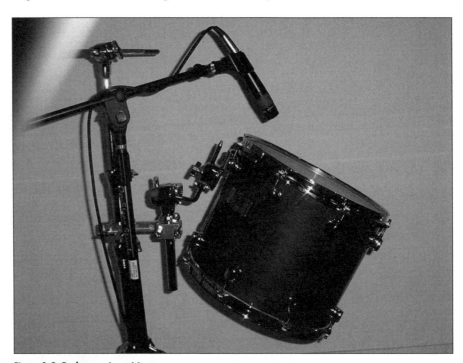

Figure 8-2: Rack tom mic position.

Figure 8-3: Tom mic positioning with a Shure KSM-44 condenser mic.

If the drummer has an especially large kit, sometimes miking each pair of toms may work better than miking each one individually. You'll need the drummer to sound check these toms and you'll need to adjust the position to get your proper blend of the two toms on this one mic.

One thing to take into consideration is the placement of all the tom mics in relation to one another. It's best if they face the same direction as much as possible. For example, looking down from the ceiling, they should all be pointing to a six o'clock position (see Figure 8-4).

Figure 8-4: Tom mics pointing in the same direction to avoid phase cancellation.

Try to avoid having one mic facing at six o'clock and another mic facing at ten o'clock or you'll most likely have phase cancellation issues between the different elements of your drum kit (see Figure 8-5).

Listen to all the tom-tom mics together, monitoring in mono as the drummer plays each one, then swap each mic's phase and listen to the difference. You might be surprised at what happens when you reverse the phase on just one mic. As before, select the position with the fullest sound.

Figure 8-5: Tom mics that can cause phase cancellation.

Tips and Tricks

Sometimes placing the mic between the tuning lugs can get a truer sound from the drum than if it's over a lug as it's slightly less constricted in that position.

FLOOR TOM MIC POSITIONING

As with the rack toms, place the mic about three inches (10 cm) above the drum head, just over the rim, pointing toward the center of the head to get the most attack. If you really need more isolation, place the mic a little closer to the head.

Although it might seem a little counterintuitive, sometimes the greatest rejection from the rest of the kit comes if the mic is placed under the ride cymbal (see Figure 8-6).

Figure 8-6: Miking the floor tom.

TOM SOUND CHECK

As with the other drums, have the drummer begin by hitting each tom at one-second intervals. Balance the gain for each one so they're all equal.

A great balanced tom mix has all the toms sounding the same, and although this comes mostly from tuning, small adjustments can also be made with EQ. For more attack, add a little bit of EQ at 5kHz and a little at 8kHz for presence. Be careful when adding the 8kHz, since it will also increase the cymbal leakage.

Attenuating the 1.5kHz range slightly decreases the "thickness" of the drum, while attenuating the 400 to 500Hz range will decrease any "boxiness" that the drum may have. On the rack toms, fullness comes at 100Hz to about 130Hz, while this occurs at around 60 to 100Hz on the floor tom.

Because the tom-tom mics are so close to the cymbals, any high frequency EQ you add to them will also add overtones from the cymbals that leak into the tom-tom channels, which is why it's always better to get the drum to sound great acoustically instead of using excessive amounts of EQ.

CHAPTER NINE
OVERHEAD MICS

Overhead mics can actually be used to capture the entire drum kit or just the cymbals, depending upon the placement. The technique you choose largely depends upon the sound you're looking for and the genre of music.

That's why there's such a variety of miking positions and philosophies when it comes specifically to overhead miking. Regardless of the technique you choose, pay close attention to the sound that the overheads supply, because it will have a great bearing on the overall sound of the drum kit.

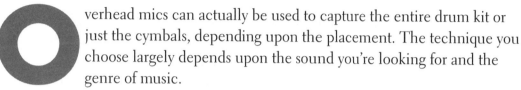

Overhead Mic Equipment Checklist:

✓ Two condenser or ribbon mics
✓ Two large mic boom stands with long arms

MICROPHONE CHOICE
Industry Standard: Royer R-121, AKG C12 or C12a, AKG 414
Popular Alternative: Neumann U87, Shure SM81, AKG 451, Royer SF-12, Shure KSM44, Coles 4038, Beyer M160, AT4040/4050, Oktava MC012
Inexpensive Substitute: MXL XL2003

Condenser and ribbon mics are almost universally favored as overheads because of their ability to faithfully capture the transient attack of the cymbals. Most engineers would opt to use vintage microphones like the AKG C12 or C12a, or the Coles 4038 for this role given the choice, but most home studio owners couldn't afford a pair of these even if they found some for sale.

Newer mics that are often used as overheads include the AKG 414 series, the AT4040/4050, or a modern ribbon mic like the

Royer R-121. Of course, less expensive mics can also be used with great success, provided you have a well-tuned kit and the right placement.

If using condenser mics, switch on the -10dB pad (if available), as the output will probably be high and may overload the microphone's internal preamp or the microphone preamp it's plugged into. On many condenser mics there is also an option to filter out lower frequencies, usually from 40Hz to around 120Hz (the frequency is different on each mic), which you may want to insert as well (see Figure 7-2). This high-pass filter can clean up the ambient sound of the kit and clarify the sound of the cymbals.

Many engineers prefer to use a stereo mic as an overhead, which makes placement much easier since there's only a single mic stand involved. One of the greatest hassles of overhead placement comes from moving the mic stands in order to align the mics correctly. A stereo mic also means that the sound is smoother from left to right because the mic's capsules are balanced more closely, frequency-wise, than two individual mics.

OVERHEAD OR CYMBAL MIC?

Overhead mics actually represent two different philosophies in drum miking. A true overhead mic is placed over the top of the drummer and is used to capture the sound of the entire kit. The individual drum mics are used more to fill in the sound and compensate for the different levels and tones of the drums in the mix.

Overhead mics are frequently used more as cymbal mics, placed directly over the cymbals to capture more of their sound than the rest of the kit. Although the cymbal mics will also capture some of the other drums as well, the cymbals will be the loudest due to the close placement of the mics.

On other occasions it might be best to "close mike" the cymbals for individual control. In this case, place a mic about six to ten inches directly over the bell of each cymbal at a 90° angle to the cymbal. There will be a limited amount of drum leakage into these mics at this position.

As mentioned in chapter two, sometimes your miking options are limited due to a low ceiling in the tracking room, which means that you're left with miking the cymbals in order to keep the mics from getting too close to the ceiling.

MIKING THE CYMBALS

To use the overheads as cymbal mics, start by putting the left and right mics parallel to each other over the crash cymbal on each side of the drum kit (see Figure 9-1).

Figure 9-1: Overhead mic positioning #1.

Place the front of the mic about twelve to eighteen inches (38–51 cm) high, pointing down over the bell of the crash cymbal (see Figure 9-2).

If the mic is placed over the edge of the cymbal instead of the bell, a "swishing" sound might be captured as the cymbal rocks back and forth and gets closer and farther away from the mic (see Figure 9-3).

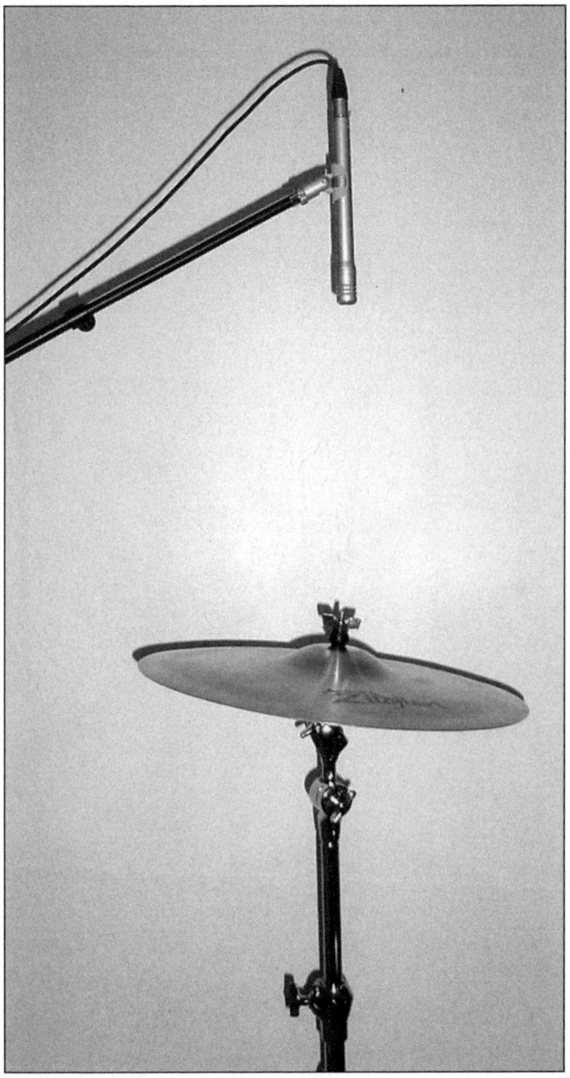

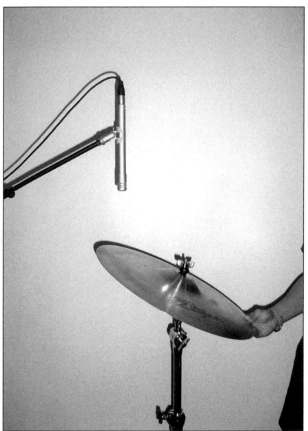

Figure 9-2: Overhead mic pointed at cymbal bell.

Figure 9-3: Placing the mic too close to the cymbal edge.

If there are two or more crash cymbals, center the mic between the crashes and raise it to diminish the swishing problem.

The ride cymbal normally cuts through everything, but if it happens to be too low in comparison with the crash cymbals, add a dedicated mic. Although you'd normally approach miking the ride the same way as the other cymbals, another way to mike it is by placing the mic underneath the cymbal pointing up at the bell from about three to six inches away. This results in the mic capturing a focused bell attack. Once again, check the phase since a mic under the kit might need to have its phase reversed.

Don't expect totally isolated tracks from the cymbal mics because there will always be leakage from the rest of the drum kit. You'll find that the snare drum especially will change when the cymbal mics or overheads are brought into the mix, which is perfectly normal. In fact, it will usually sound a lot more natural as a result.

OVERHEAD MIC POSITION #1

While the previous setup is used mainly for miking the cymbals, overhead position #1 is designed to capture the sound of the entire drum kit. In this configuration, two mics are crossed at a 110° angle (see Figure 9-4) and about seven inches apart.

This is sometimes mistakenly called "XY" but the official name is "ORTF," which is the technique developed and adopted by the Radio and Television Organization of France. The angle of 110° was chosen because it's the same as the ear spacing on your head and produces a highly localized stereo soundfield and a greater sense of space as a result.

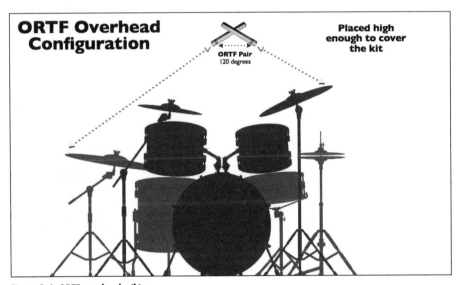

Figure 9-4: ORTF overhead miking.

The trick to this overhead technique is that it becomes the main sound of the kit with the other mics just filling in and reinforcing it. It also allows you to use a lot fewer mics, something that we'll discuss further in chapter eleven.

Tips and Tricks

If you have a room that's too live, move the overheads closer to the kit to reduce the amount of room being picked up. This will also increase the presence and clarity of the other drums leaking into the overheads.

OVERHEAD MIC POSITION #2

A variation on overhead position #1 is to use an X/Y microphone pair about two feet over the drummer's head, centered over the middle of the kit (see Figure 9-5). The X/Y configuration occurs when the capsules nearly touch at a 90° angle. Raise or lower the mics to achieve the desired kit balance, as well as the balance between the amount of room sound and the direct sound of the kit.

Figure 9-5: XY overhead miking.

Although the difference doesn't seem to be very large between the two miking positions, many engineers prefer the stereo image of the XY configuration to the ORTF used in Position #1. That said, it really is a matter of taste as the results are similar.

OVERHEAD SOUND CHECK

While many engineers automatically pan the overheads hard left and hard right for the most dramatic effect, most pro mixers are much more conservative, since a drum sound that wide could sound unnatural. It's not uncommon to see panning at nine o'clock and three o'clock or even more towards the center, since that emphasizes the drum kit as a single instrument as opposed to a collection of individual drums and cymbals, and better approximates how the kit is actually heard in real life.

To check the cymbal balance, have the drummer hit the crash cymbals on the left and then the right side of the kit and set the levels so that each side is equal. Another way to check the levels is to have the drummer hit the snare and listen to be sure that its ambience is heard just a little to the right of center through the two overhead mics.

Be sure that the recording level isn't too high (about -10dB to -5dBFS on the DAW meters). It's just as important to leave some headroom on digital gear as it is on analog since the high-frequency transients that the cymbals produce may not be picked up by the meters.

If you find a particular cymbal is standing out, move the mic away from that cymbal. If one cymbal seems lost, move the mic a bit closer to it. Although the ride cymbal will usually be picked up from all the other open drum mics, you might have to add an additional spot mic on it. This is especially true if the drummer's crash cymbals are thicker, and therefore louder, than the ride.

Have the drummer play a song that features each piece of the kit so you can check the kit balance. You should hear an even balance of the kit, although you may want to slightly adjust the overhead mic position if something seems to be standing out or being lost.

> ### Tips and Tricks
> Sometimes just asking the drummer to hit a drum or cymbal harder is a lot easier than adjusting the level or EQ, but make sure this approach fits the song.

Many cymbals can use a touch of 8–10kHz EQ to make them sparkle, while others may need a decrease at 160–200Hz to lower the *clang* sound.

CHAPTER TEN
ROOM MICS

Room mics bring an overall polish to the drum sound and help to glue it all together. In many cases, they'll fill in the sonic holes in the drum mix and make all the individual drums sound more like a complete drum set.

Room Mic Checklist:

✓ Stereo mic or two condenser mics with cables
✓ Either one or two mic stands

MICROPHONE CHOICE
Industry Standard: AKG C24 (VERY expensive choice and hard to find but #1 on the list)
Popular Choice: Rode NT4
Inexpensive Substitute: Two MXL XL2003s, Shure VP88

The choice of microphones in this application depends upon the sound of the room. If the room is dark, then a brighter mic will accentuate the high end. If the room is relatively smooth sounding, then a more neutral mic like the Shure VP-88 stereo mic works well, as does the vintage AKG C-24 and Neumann SM69 (if you can afford them).

Consider what you're trying to achieve when using room mics. If the goal is to capture more of the room ambience, then a single mic pointing away from the drums might work well. If the goal is to get a bigger drum sound, place a mic (or mics) at the point in the room where the kit seems most balanced.

You might try using a figure-8 pattern if you have a mic with that polar pattern (like a ribbon mic). This could work better as a room mic in a small room because the mic will pick up the reflections from the back wall, but not the side-to-side or floor-to-ceiling reflections that sometimes sound bad. Even if the mic is angled it will still pick up fewer of these reflections than any other pattern. As a result, where a small room may add an unpleasant sound when recorded with omnis or cardioids, it may sound perfectly acceptable with a figure 8.

> ### Tips and Tricks
>
> Generally speaking, the fewer mics used to close-mike the drums, the more effective the room mics will be.

ROOM MIC POSITION #1

The better the drum kit sounds, the more this configuration will add to the sound of the drums. It's an easy setup as well.

Place a stereo mic placed about six feet in front of the drum kit at about six or seven feet high. Angle the mic down at a 45° angle towards the middle of the kit.

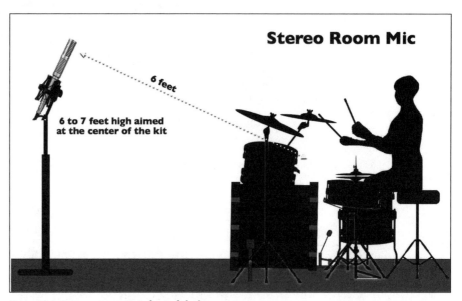

Stereo Room Mic

6 feet

6 to 7 feet high aimed at the center of the kit

Figure 10-1: Using a stereo mic in front of the kit.

Room Mic Position #1 Alternate

Any mic will work in this position if a stereo mic isn't available. While many engineers prefer a large diaphragm condenser microphone for this purpose, even an SM57 can do a superb job of capturing the overall sound of the kit.

ROOM MIC POSITION #2

Another method for room miking in a small room is to place the stereo mic directly over the kit, centering on the middle of the bass drum about six feet above. This is in addition to the cymbal mics.

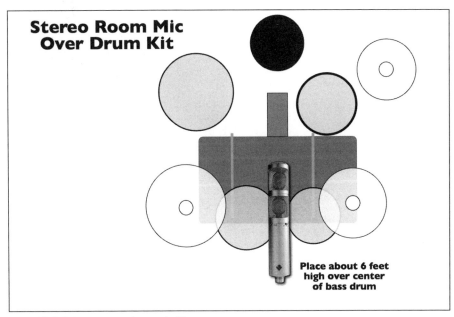

Stereo Room Mic Over Drum Kit

Place about 6 feet high over center of bass drum

Figure 10-2: Using a stereo mic over the kit.

ROOM MIC POSITION #3

Another effective room miking configuration is parallel miking. Place a mic at each side of the kit about ten feet apart and looking directly at the outside edge of the farthest cymbal. The mics should be between six to ten feet in front of the kit, and should sit just on the edge of the kit on the same plane and exactly parallel to each other.

The distance is determined by the balance of the kit. Place the mics at the spot where the kit is most balanced. Another placement technique in a larger room is to place the mics where the room ambience matches the level of the drums sound itself.

This technique might seem like you're miking the wall behind the drum kit, but it will give you both the sound of the room reflections and the kit. By keeping the mics parallel, phase shift is kept to a minimum.

> ### *Tips and Tricks*
> Draw a vertical line between the bass drum and the snare drum and use that as a center point for your parallel room mics.

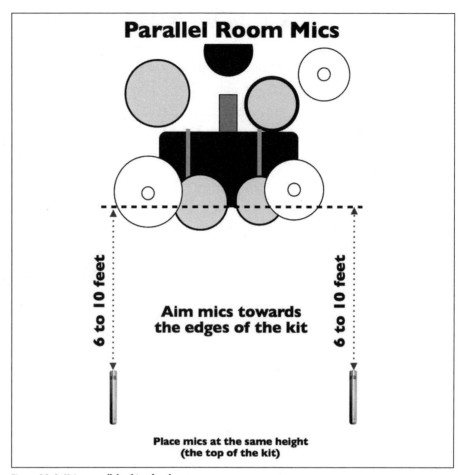

Figure 10-3: Using parallel miking for the room.

For any of these methods, *do not* engage the low-frequency roll-off on the mic if it has one. Capturing the full-frequency spectrum will fill in any of the holes you might get from the other mics on the kit. You'll find that the low end of the room mics can make the kick sound bigger and deeper as the low frequencies take a bit of distance to develop.

ROOM MIC SOUND CHECK

If using a stereo mic or a pair of room mics panned in stereo, begin by having the drummer hit the snare drum and adjust the levels on the mic preamps so each channel is equal. If the levels between the mics are balanced, then the snare should be panned off to the right a little, at about 12:30, which is where the snare sits in relation to the kit. Ask the drummer to hit all the cymbals and the kick drum to make sure that nothing is peaking the meters, then ask him to play the song you plan on recording to be sure that the mics or mic preamps don't overload.

Depending on the room, you might want to add 2 or 3dB of 12 or 14kHz to open up the sound of the room and give it a little "air." If the room already has a bright sound, this may not be necessary. Some engineers will insert the high-pass filter to reduce the low end from the room mics while others use the sound of the low end of room mics to add bottom or deepen the toms if that's needed to help the drum mix later on.

While it's popular to heavily compress room mics during the mix to emphasize the ambience of the room, it's best not to add any compression while recording, since it can't be changed later.

Tips and Tricks

Not cutting low frequencies from the room mics can save you later. I was doing a jazz session with Gary Novack once where it was being recorded to tape. When the assistant transferred the tape tracks over to Pro Tools later, kick drum track didn't make it thanks to a bad electronics card that we found out about later. I was able to save the session by boosting 50Hz on the room mic tracks by 8dB. This won't work for every kind of music, but it sure worked in this case.

—Dennis Moody

CHAPTER ELEVEN
ALTERNATIVE MIKING TECHNIQUES

Remember all those great old Led Zeppelin and Beach Boys records your grandma played? These are great examples of what can be done with the limited technology they had back in the 1960s as compared to what's available today.

This section will show some of those alternative miking techniques that you might want to try if you have a limited amount of gear, or just don't want to be bothered with the more involved multiple mic setup that's been described so far in this book. These are some simple tried-and-true ways that you've no doubt heard on many hit records through the years.

Microphone Choice

Popular Mic Choice: Any condenser mic, Shure SM57 or Shure SM58

Having a $6,000 vintage Neumann tube mic is probably going to sound better than a $29 low-quality mic in many of the following techniques, but you'd be surprised how much the sound can change by just varying the placement, compression, and EQ.

Proper placement is everything, so don't worry if all you have available is a few SM58s that you use onstage.

SINGLE MIC TECHNIQUE

If you've ever recorded a band rehearsal, at some point you've probably experimented with using a single microphone on the drums. However, there are some tricks to getting the best drum sound out of only one mic.

If you put a mic about three feet (1 m) in front of the drum set looking at the center of the kit, you'll find that it should pick up everything fairly evenly (see Figure 11-1).

Listen while the drummer is playing a song using the entire kit and have someone move the mic around until you find a position that gets an even balance of all the drums and cymbals. If you need more bass drum, move the mic down slightly toward the bass drum. If you need a little less, move it higher and away from the bass drum. You can also pull the bass drum up in the mix by adding a few dB at 60Hz.

Figure 11-1: Single mic technique.

With a single mic on the drums, a bit of compression can help smooth out the dynamics of the kit. Start with a fairly light setting just to reign in the peaks—minus a dB or two with a 2:1 ratio and the fastest attack and release settings available. Don't be afraid to experiment with over-compressing as you may find you like the wild effect that it sometimes achieves.

TWO MIC TECHNIQUE

If you have two mics available, try placing one in front of the bass drum about six inches (18 cm) away from the front head and positioning the second mic up about two and a half feet (90 cm) above the kit as an overhead (about a foot over the drummer's head), looking down at the middle of the kit (see Figure 11-2). This configuration will give you a mono recording.

Figure 11-2: Two mic technique.

While the drummer is playing, have someone move the overhead mic around until the kit sounds balanced. If the snare isn't loud enough, for example, move the mic a little more towards the snare, and if you're getting too much, move it the other way. A little equalization at 12kHz can give the kit a bit more clarity and crispness.

This is the classic method that was used on so many hits back in the '60s. Go online and take a look at some photos of old Led Zeppelin or The Who recording sessions. You'll see some great examples of two-mic drum recording.

THREE MIC TECHNIQUE

Three mics actually provide two mic positioning choices. The first option is use the two-mic configuration as described above, but add a third mic for the snare drum. Position this snare mic as described earlier in the book in the snare-miking chapter (see Figure 11-3).

To capture more hi-hat, move the snare drum mic about two inches (7 cm) away from the snare and a bit more towards the hat. This configuration will give you a mono recording only.

Three Mic Technique Option Two

For a stereo recording using only three mics, try option two, which uses one bass drum mic and two overheads. Place these overhead mics about two and a half feet (90 cm) over the left and right sides of the kit pointed straight down at a 90° angle to the floor (see Figure 11-4).

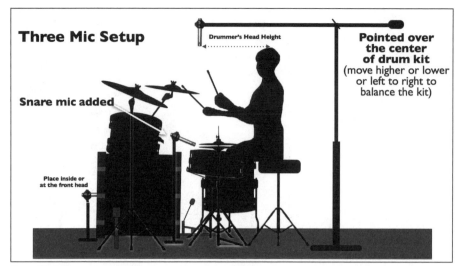

Figure 11-3: Three mic technique.

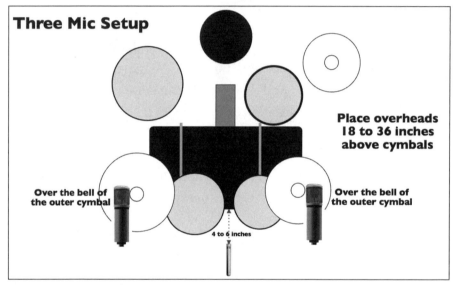

Figure 11-4: Option two—three mic technique.

Again, move the mics as needed in order to either change the balance, or improve the stereo imaging.

Three Mic Technique Option Three

This method may be the oddest-looking and non-intuitive option when using three mics, but it has a unique place in recording history and really does work.

It starts off just like the two mic technique, with a single overhead and kick drum mic, but adds a third mic a few feet above the floor tom pointing across the kit towards the snare. It's strange, but the story behind it will explain it a bit better (see Figure 11-5).

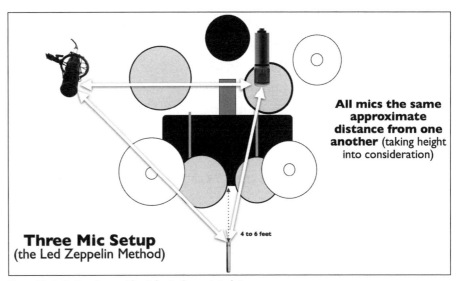

All mics the same approximate distance from one another (taking height into consideration)

Three Mic Setup
(the Led Zeppelin Method)

4 to 6 feet

Figure 11-5: Option three—Glyn Johns's three mic technique.

This technique was accidentally stumbled upon by the famous engineer/producer Glyn Johns while recording the second Led Zeppelin record. John Bonham's drums at the time were being recorded in mono with just an overhead and kick drum mic, when Johns sent an assistant out to the studio to change the settings on Jimmy Page's guitar amp. The assistant moved the mic while changing the settings and forgot to move it back. Meanwhile, the mic came to rest at the side of the floor tom pointing towards the snare. When Bonham started to play again, everyone in the control room was floored with the huge sound they heard. And it was in stereo, which is the first known occasion of stereo drums! Johns went on to use the technique on classic records with The Who, Rod Stewart, The Rolling Stones, The Eagles, and still uses a version of it today.

What to remember is that the kick drum mic used in the original version of the technique was really a "drum front" mic as it was placed about six feet away from the kick where it hears all the drums equally. That said, you might want to place the kick drum mic as described in the bass drum chapter for a more modern sound.

Another thing to remember is that the overhead and side mics should be about the same distance from the snare.

FOUR MIC TECHNIQUE

The four mic technique is the same as option two mentioned in the three mic technique, but with the addition of a snare drum mic. Position the snare drum mic as described in chapter six.

This is a great technique for jazz or any type of music requiring an open, natural sound (see Figure 11-6).

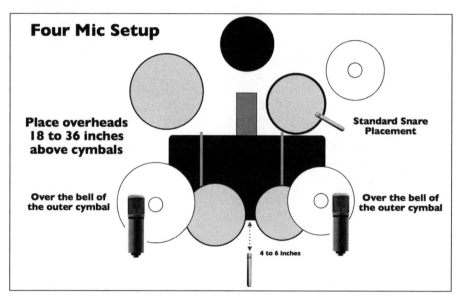

Four Mic Setup

Place overheads 18 to 36 inches above cymbals

Standard Snare Placement

Over the bell of the outer cymbal

Over the bell of the outer cymbal

4 to 6 inches

Figure 11-6: Four mic technique, option one.

Four Mic Technique Option Two

In this technique, the kick and snare mics stay the same but the overheads are placed in a crossing ORTF configuration (remember chapter seven on overheads?). Place them about six or seven feet above the kit directly in the middle. You can also use the "X/Y" mic positioning on the overheads as well. You may prefer it over the ORTF configuration. A bit of experimenting will get you to where you want to be with the four mic drum method.

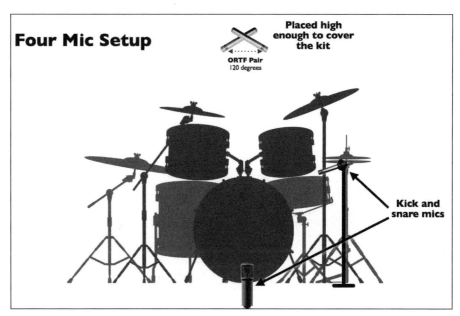

Figure 11-7: Four mic technique, option two.

As you can see, there are lots of options without having to resort to miking every drum and cymbal. The best part is that all of these techniques really work, the proof being the many great records they've been used on over the years.

CHAPTER TWELVE

GETTING THE DRUM MIX TOGETHER

n just about any popular music, the drum sound is of vital importance to the overall mix of the song. Have a wimpy drum sound and the entire mix will take on that character. That's why it's important to have a great sounding drum mix before just about anything else.

In the early days of recording there wasn't much of a drum mix since the entire kit was treated as a single instrument and miked with just a single mic. As producers began to understand how important the beat was, a mic was added to the kick. Eventually the modern drum sound evolved to the point that each drum (and sometimes each cymbal) is individually miked. As a result, the internal mix of the drums is a vital part of virtually every modern recording.

HAVE A LISTEN

Once you've miked your individual drums in a way you like, it's time to listen to the kit as a whole.

First, stand about five to ten feet (2–4 m) in front of the kit and listen to the balance while the drummer plays, then go back in front of your speakers and listen to him play again. Does the mix have the same balance as when you were standing in front of the kit?

The idea is to balance the mix of the drum mics to achieve the same blend that you were hearing acoustically first, then enhance it later as needed.

> ### Tips and Tricks
> Ask the drummer to play the song that you'll be recording instead of just flailing around the drums like some drummers like to do. It will give you a better idea of how the drum kit sounds.

BALANCING THE DRUM KIT

The best way to approach creating a drum mix is to think of the drum kit as one instrument, not seven or eight separate elements.

Listen for a unified overall sound with no one element standing out from the rest. Hearing "lead hi-hat" or "lead tom-tom" can be very distracting to your audience and take all the pleasure out of listening to the recording—unless, of course, that's an effect that you trying to achieve.

The drum mix is all about balance—balance between all the drum mics and then balance of the drum mix itself against the rest of the band.

There are several schools of thought on where to start your mix. Many engineers begin with the kick, although some start from the overheads, and still others from the toms. Regardless of where you start, the idea is exactly the same—to blend all the different drum mics into a cohesive single drum sound.

Drum Kit Balance Technique One

Step 1: If the kit was recorded with the overheads miking the cymbals more than the entire kit, bring the fader of the kick drum up first so that the meter reads about -10 on the peaks. At this point, you might want to add a little compression (1dB or so) to even out the peaks. If you want a more aggressive kick sound you can add more compression later after the entire kit is balanced.

> *Tips and Tricks*
>
> Try to refrain from adding any EQ at this time, since this is something best left until after the whole kit is balanced. You may need to add some high mid-frequencies to make the kick cut through the mix. If you listen to the kick by itself with this extra EQ, it may sound too sharp, but you'll find that it's perfect in the mix blend.

Step 2: Bring up the snare until it's at about the same level as the kick. Again, you may want to add a little compression to even out the peaks.

Step 3: Bring up the hat and toms to a level that matches what you heard, acoustically, in the room. Make sure that the level of each tom is the same on any tom fill that might happen during the song. (If that's not happening, you may have to automate some of the fills.)

Step 4: Bring the overheads up until you can just hear them. Make sure the cymbals are not overpowering the rest of the kit. The only way to know that is to have all the drum mics in the mix, since they all have a little cymbal in them.

Step 5: Finally, bring up the room mics to the point where you can just hear them. This will fill in the sound and glue the kit balance together.

It's popular in rock to heavily compress the room mics to bring out the ambience of the room and add a natural reverb, but this only works if the sound of the room is good to begin with. Heavy compression also changes the balance between the drums and cymbals, which come to the forefront and usually become too loud. (Compression is discussed in more depth later in the chapter.)

Drum Kit Balance Technique Two
If your overheads are there to pick up the sound of the entire kit, then the mix is approached differently, since they then become the main source of the kit's sound.

Step 1: Bring up the faders on the overheads so that the meters read about -10dBFS at the peaks. The drum sound should already sound fairly balanced.

Step 2: Bring up each drum track until you can just hear it. The idea is to fill in the sound and add some punch. When you add the rest of the instruments, you'll probably have to add a bit more of the drums, especially the kick and snare.

Drum Kit Balance Technique Three
This technique is used when the tom fills are especially prominent in the song.

Step 1: Start by bringing the tom faders up until the meters read about -10dBFS at the peaks. Make sure the level and the sound of all of the toms are pretty much the same by adding or subtracting EQ as needed.

If a tom needs more attack then add a bit of 5k to bring that out, or a bit of 100Hz if it needs more body, as mentioned in the chapter on tom recording. Go through the song to make sure that every fill is balanced, automating the toms that are too loud or too quiet as needed.

Step 2: Build the mix around the toms, starting from whichever drum mic you're comfortable with.

Setting the Levels

Regardless of where you start your mix, keep in mind that the mix buss level will increase with the introduction of every new track or element. That's why it's best to begin your mix with the mix buss meter (the master meters) reading at about -10dB, regardless of the instrument you start off with. With each instrument that enters at the same level as the current mix, the master mix meter should raise about 3dB.

Also remember that the sound of every drum will change anywhere from a little to a lot when a new drum or cymbal is added to the mix due to the leakage of the other drums into the mic. This may be especially noticeable on the snare drum, but usually for the better, as the snare becomes more natural sounding without having to use the EQ.

CHECKING THE DRUM PHASE

We've already discussed the importance of checking the phase during recording, but this is a good time to check it one more time before the mix goes any further.

Step 1: With all the drums in the mix, go to the kick drum channel and change the selection of the polarity or phase control. Is there more low end or less? Choose the selection with the most bottom end. You'll find this phase difference easier to hear if you listen to the recording in mono.

Step 2: Go to the snare drum channel and change the selection of the polarity or phase control. Is there more low end or less? Choose the selection with the most bottom end.

Step 3: Go to each tom mic channel and change the selection of the polarity or phase control. Is there more low end or less? Choose the selection with the most bottom end.

Step 4: Go to each cymbal mic or overhead mic and change the selection of the polarity or phase control. Is there more low end or less? Choose the selection with the most bottom end.

DRUM MIX PANNING

Back in the days when a drum kit was recorded with only a few microphones, the drums were recorded in mono, sometimes on a single track, but—more often than not—mixed together with the other instruments. Today, with most drum kits and drum loops tracked in stereo, the entire mix is built upon the idea that the drums will take up space in the stereo field.

There are two approaches to panning the drums. Most mixers will pan it the way they see the kit setup (known as "audience perspective"), with the hi-hat slightly on the right and floor tom on the left for a right-handed player. A few mixers choose to pan from the drummer's perspective, where everything is reversed.

As stated previously, the tendency is to pan the overheads and room mics hard left and hard right for a very wide stereo field. That might work on some songs, but the current trend is to pan the drums in closer to the center at about nine o'clock and three o'clock or even more to the center, to give them the feel of a single instrument. Wide panning can sometimes be distracting, especially in a song with a lot of wide-panned tom fills.

You can even try panning the individual recorded drum tracks to the center, then add a wide-panned room mic or overheads. This method was used on many popular recordings coming out of San Francisco in the late '70s and early '80s. It creates a really compact sound, yet still feels spacious.

EQUALIZING THE DRUMS

The drums present an interesting dilemma—does the song demand that the drum kit work as a whole, or should the snare or kick stand out? Once again, it depends on the song, but it's important to be aware of both approaches.

The kick and snare are extremely important in modern music because the kick is the heartbeat and the snare drives the song. By simply getting the sound and balance of these two drums right, it's possible to change a song from dull to exciting.

There are certain frequencies on different drums that make a big difference in how each sounds in the drum mix.

Kick: Bottom at 80–100Hz, hollowness at 400Hz, point at 3–5kHz, and presence at 8kHz

Snare: Fatness at 90–140Hz, point at 900Hz to 1.4kHz, crispness at 5kHz, presence at 10–14kHz

Hat: Clang at 200Hz, sparkle at 8–12kHz

Rack Toms: Fullness at 100–140Hz, attack at 3.5–6kHz

Floor Tom: Fullness at 80Hz, attack at 5kHz

Cymbals: Clang at 200Hz, sparkle at 8–12kHz

These frequencies are not cut and dried for each drum kit, since the size of the drum or cymbal and the material they're made of, as well as their quality, contribute greatly to the tone. Remember to sweep the frequencies around each of the above to find the frequency for that particular drum or cymbal that brings a sound to your liking.

Also be aware that boosting from 40–60Hz may make the kick sound big on your speakers, but it might not be heard when played back on smaller speakers. The ideal spot for a 22" kick drum (which is the most commonly used) is around 80Hz.

ADDING ARTIFICIAL AMBIENCE TO THE DRUM KIT

Ideally, the drum ambience will come from the reflections in the tracking room that are picked up by the room mics, but sometimes the room is too small, sounds bad or the decay time is too short, so it must be augmented.

The drum kit is different from the other instruments in the mix in that it may use several different reverbs in order for it to lay correctly in the track. For instance, the kick drum may be left completely dry, while the snare drum may have its own separate reverb from what the rest of the kit uses. In fact, the cymbals and hat may also have more of a room sound, while the toms may need larger sound that puts them further back into the mix. On the other hand, a single reverb used across the kit may be just enough to make the kit sound great.

For a safe, general-purpose reverb setting that works in most situations, dial in a room or plate reverb with a twenty millisecond pre-delay and a one- to two-second decay time. For ballads, set the decay longer; for faster tunes, set it shorter. Ideally, you're trying to have the reverb tail die off by the next snare hit.

Some mixers prefer a second reverb just for the snare and maybe the toms. This is often set to non-linear, gated, or inverse room (all pretty much the same) with the same settings as the room. Once again, the idea is to have the decay die out just before the next snare hit.

ASSIGNING THE DRUMS TO A GROUP OR SUBGROUP

Sometimes it's convenient to assign some or all the drum tracks to either a group or a subgroup in order to make any mix adjustments somewhat easier.

In a group, a number of channel faders (like the drums) are electronically or digitally chained together so if you move one fader in the group, they all move, yet keep the same relative balance that you originally set. A subgroup has the same effect, yet works a little differently. All the channels of the group are assigned to a subgroup fader, and that subgroup fader's output is then assigned to the master mix buss. The level of all the assigned channels is controlled with that one fader, and if you move any fader within the group the others don't move with it, but you change the balance of the mix. If you send the subgroup to an effect, or insert a compressor on the subgroup, it also affects all the instruments in that group, which can be a benefit in certain situations during mixing.

Examples of groups might be just the overheads, all of the toms, the room mics, the top and bottom snare mics, and the inside and outside kick drum mics. For example, once you get the perfect blend of your top and bottom snare mics, assign them to a group and balance will be locked into that blend if you move either one of them up or down in the mix. Multiple drum groups may even be assigned to their own separate subgroup to make it easier to balance the drums against the rest of the mix elements.

Assigning the Drum Channels to a Subgroup

Step 1: After getting a workable blend, assign all of the drum channels to a group. Move one of the faders. Do all the faders move yet keep the same balance relationship?

Step 2: Again, after getting a blend on your console or DAW, assign all of your drum channels to a subgroup. Raise or lower the subgroup fader. Does the level of the drums get louder and softer?

COMPRESSING THE DRUMS

There are a number of reasons to compress the drums. Sometimes a drummer doesn't hit every beat on the kick and snare with the same intensity, which can make the pulse of the song feel erratic. Sometimes, the tom fills have different volumes across the drums.

In terms of using compression as an effect, it can work wonders when it seems to push the kick and snare forward in the track to make them much more punchy.

Compressing the Snare

To begin, set the Threshold control of the compressor so that no compression occurs, the Ratio set at 2:1, and the Attack and Release controls and the Output control set to mid-way.

Step 1: Solo the snare, then slowly decrease the Threshold until the Gain Reduction Meter reads 2 dB. Can you hear the compression? What does the master mix buss meter read? Can you hear a difference if you bypass the compressor?

Step 2: Increase the Attack time to as slow as it will go, then gradually increase it (make it faster) until the attack begins to dull, then back it off a hair.

Step 3: Increase the Release time to as slow as it will go, then slowly increase the Release time until the snare reaches 90 to 100 percent volume on the next snare hit.

Step 4: Select the Bypass control to hear the volume of the snare without the compressor. Now deselect the Bypass and slowly raise the

Output control (sometimes called Gain or Makeup Gain) until the compressed signal level is equal to the uncompressed signal in level. Compare these two and see what works best to your ear for your song. Sometimes using no compression at all will give the song a natural sound that will add a lot to the overall effect.

Step 5: To make the snare seem closer to you in the mix, increase the compression by increasing the Threshold or Ratio controls.

> ### Tips and Tricks
> Increasing the Ratio control will make the sound more aggressive as you'll hear the compression more.

Use the same procedure for the kick and toms.

Compressing the Room Mics

Step 1: Set the Attack time as slow as it will go, then increase it until the sound of the room just begins to dull.

Step 2: Now increase the Release time to as slow as it will go and increase it until the room reaches 90 to 100 percent volume on the next snare hit.

Step 3: Select the Bypass to hear the volume of the room without the compressor. Now deselect the Bypass and slowly raise the Output control until the compressed signal is equal to the uncompressed signal in level.

Step 4: Many mixers prefer the room sound to be extremely compressed. Increase the compression by increasing the Threshold or Ratio controls until there's about 10 dB (or more) of compression, then tuck the room tracks in just under the other drum tracks.

GATING THE DRUMS

A gate (sometimes called "Noise Gate" or "Expander") is sort of a reverse-compressor. That is, it works backwards from a normal compressor in that the sound level is at its loudest until it reaches the threshold, where it's then decreased or muted completely.

A gate can be used to cover up noises, buzzes, coughs, or other low-level sounds that were recorded on a track. For example, gates can be used to turn off the leakage from the tom mics, since having these tracks open when the toms are not being played tend to muddy up the other drum tracks.

A gate can sometimes consist of just a few controls, principally the Threshold, Range and sometimes Hold or Release controls.

Range sets the amount of attenuation after the threshold is reached and the gate turns on or "closes" the channel. Sometimes when gating drums, the Range control is set so it attenuates the signal only about 10 or 20 dB. This lets some of the natural ambience remain and prevents the drums from sounding choked.

The Hold control keeps the gate open a defined amount of time, and the Release control works just like on a compressor.

Using a Gate on the Snare Drum

Step 1: Solo the snare and insert the gate on the channel.

Step 2: Raise the Threshold control until you can hear the snare drum hit, but no sound in between hits.

Step 3: Adjust the Range control so the snare is attenuated by 10dB between hits. Increase the Range control for more isolation between hits.

Step 4: If the gate chatters, try fine-tuning the settings of the Threshold and Release controls (if the gate has one). If it still chatters, add a compressor before the gate to keep the signal steady.

Using a Gate on the Toms

Step 1: Go to a place in the song where there's a tom fill. Solo the tom and insert the gate on the channel.

Step 2: Raise the Threshold control until you can hear the tom drum hit, but no sound in between hits.

Step 3: Adjust the Range control so the tom is attenuated by 10dB between hits. Increase the Range control for more isolation between hits.

Step 4: If the gate chatters, try fine-tuning the settings of the Threshold and Release controls (if the gate has one). If it still chatters, add a compressor before the gate to keep the signal steady.

CHAPTER THIRTEEN

MIKING PERCUSSION

Percussion is much more important to the final mix of a song than many musicians and engineers think. In fact, it's responsible for the motion of many hit songs, and without it the feel would change completely.

Some percussion is mixed low in the track but still makes a difference in a song's movement, even in a genre like rock or country where percussion isn't normally expected. Take it away and the motion stops.

Microphone Choice

Popular Choice: Large or small diaphragm condenser mic, ribbon mic

Just like the drums, percussion can be difficult to capture due to the highly transient nature of the attacks. That's why a condenser or ribbon mic works well to record this class of instruments, since they have a response fast enough to capture those short energy bursts. Sometimes a dynamic mic is a better choice if the instrument is too bright, as its slower transient response smooths out the response.

THE TWO PERCUSSION GROUPS

Percussion can be categorized into two groups: the low-frequency drum-style instruments like bongos, congas, djembe (see Figure 13-5), and udu; and high-frequency hand-held instruments like shakers, tambourines, and triangles. Because these two groups of instruments are so different, they each require a different recording approach.

Recording Drum Percussion

For drum percussion, it's important that they're tuned first. (See chapter one on drum tuning, and use the same technique.) For the best sound possible, it's also important to have a good-sounding room with a hard floor. Most percussionists will want to set up their congas or djembe on a piece of plywood if there is no hardwood floor. This will add to the resonance of the drum and will enhance your recording.

While dynamic mics are often used on congas and "drum style" percussion, condenser mics can better capture the sound of the instrument because of their quick reaction time that captures the transients of the instrument.

As a general rule, here's a good way to begin miking drum-style percussion.

Step 1: Using a single mic, place it about twelve inches over the drum, aimed towards the middle of the head (see Figure 13-1). For two drums, like congas, place the mic between the drums but aim it slightly towards the drum that's lower tuned.

Step 2: Put a finger in your ear and walk around the instrument. Is there a particular place where it sounds better?

Step 3: Place the mic where the acoustic sound of the drum has the best combination of tone and balance of direct to ambient sound.

Figure 13-1: Miking drum percussion.

Recording Hand-Held Percussion

Hand-held percussion, like shakers and tambourines, have always been a big part of the rhythm section as they're responsible for adding motion to the song. For example, back in the '60s, most R&B records would actually have a tambourine louder in the track than the drums.

There are a number of things to consider when recording them, though. First, the instrument must be moved when playing, so close-miking usually won't work. And second, the transient response of most hand-held instruments puts added strain on the entire signal chain, so it's always best to record with extra headroom.

Step 1: Place a condenser mic set to an omni pattern about five feet away at about head level, but pointing down at the instrument (see Figure 13-2).

Step 2: Adjust the level of the mic amp so the meter on the DAW reads about -10dB (or lower) on peaks. If you're getting too much ambience, have the player move closer to the mic but not closer than one to two feet away. You'll get the full spectrum of the percussion sound this way as long as the percussionist doesn't move off mic too much.

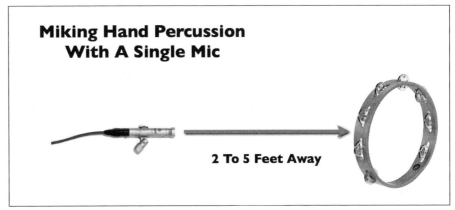

Miking Hand Percussion With A Single Mic

2 To 5 Feet Away

Figure 13-2: Miking hand percussion.

RECORDING SPECIFIC PERCUSSION INSTRUMENTS

Here are a number of common percussion instruments along with the most popular microphone placement to capture them faithfully.

Conga

For congas, a hard floor in a fairly large room is beneficial to getting a good, natural sound. A hardwood floor is the best, but tile or linoleum will do. If you don't have a floor with a hard surface, then use the plywood trick mentioned above.

Placement: Place a small diaphragm condenser or dynamic mic about one to two inches in from the outer rim, and hovering about twelve inches above each drum (see Figure 13-3).

Figure 13-3: AKG 452 over the conga.

Cowbell

Cowbells project a high-frequency transient from the closed end as well as a fundamental frequency from the open end. Keep in mind, however, that while the high end of the cowbell easily cuts through the mix, the low frequencies occasionally get lost.

Placement: Place a mic about two feet in front on the cowbell but about a foot above it and angled downward (see Figure 13-4). You may have to add a dB or two at 3kHz to get it to cut through the track if you have a dull-sounding cowbell.

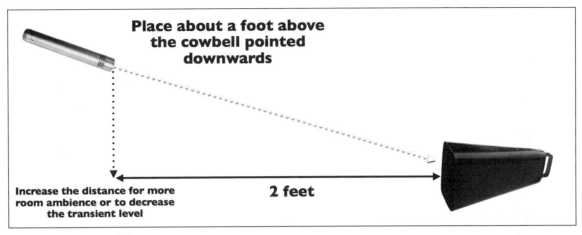

Place about a foot above the cowbell pointed downwards

Increase the distance for more room ambience or to decrease the transient level

2 feet

Figure 13-4: Miking a cowbell.

Djembe

The heads on most djembes are fairly wide (fourteen inches or so), but most of the bass sound comes from the bottom of the instrument and not from the head. There really isn't a single spot close to the drum where a mic can capture the full djembe sound, however, so some distance is required during mic placement. Often a bottom mic is added to record a djembe, but be sure to check the phase if you choose to add one.

Placement: In a good-sounding room, the drum should be miked from six to ten feet away (see Figure 13-5).

Figure 13-5: Mic placed over a djembe.

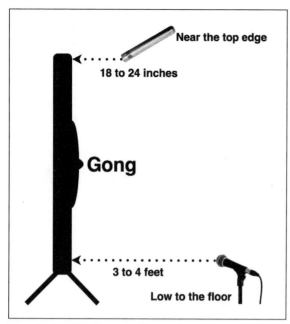

Figure 13-6: Miking the gong with two mics.

Gong

A gong has a thunderous low end, so a cardioid mic with proximity effect will make it sound muddy. Try a mic with an omni pattern instead.

Placement: Place a dynamic mic low to the floor and about four feet away to capture the low end, and a small diaphragm omni condenser near the top of the gong about eighteen inches away to capture the harmonics (see Figure 13-6).

Handclaps

Handclaps are best done in a group, with the more clappers, the better. Claps are often augmented with foot stomps, boards, or electronic claps to achieve the proper effect.

Placement: Claps need distance to develop, so start with a dynamic mic (to smooth out the transients) at least three feet away (see Figure 13-7). You may want to add some limiting or compression to the recorded track to get them as even as possible as the dynamic range of group handclaps is very broad.

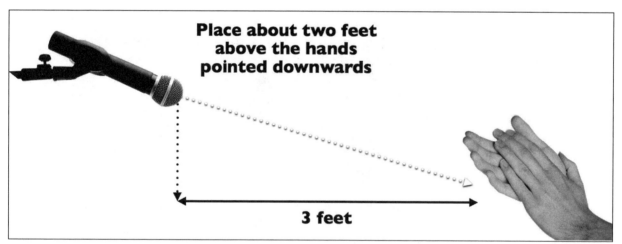

Figure 13-7: Miking handclaps.

Shaker

Shakers have become a vital part of the rhythm section in popular music, as they subtly add motion to a song. Many drummers and percussionists use a wide variety of shakers, both store-bought and home-made.

Placement: Set a condenser mic to omni and place it two to three feet away from the shaker, at about head level (see Figure 13-8).

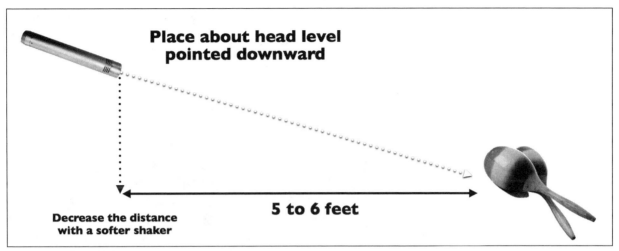

Place about head level pointed downward

Decrease the distance with a softer shaker

5 to 6 feet

Figure 13-8: Miking a shaker.

Tips and Tricks

Sometimes some salt inside two Styrofoam drinking cups taped together will sit better in the track than a real shaker. This will give you a soft sound that may be perfect for your song. You can also try rice or even popcorn kernels to get a heavier and brighter sound.

Tambourine

Place your tambourine player in the most ambient, brightest part of your recording room. Keep in mind that since a tambourine must be moved when playing, close-miking might pick up a lot of air noise or movement from the percussionist.

Placement: Place a mic with an omni pattern two to four feet away, at about head level (see Figure 13-9).

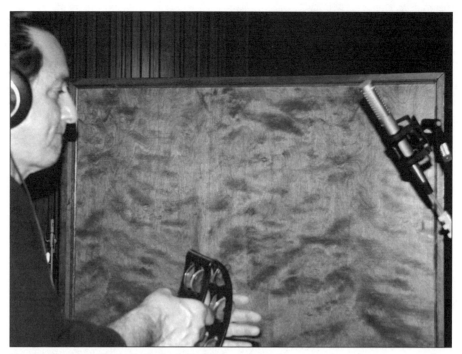

Figure 13-9: A Royer R-121 placed on a tambourine.

Tips and Tricks

Sometimes a really dark-sounding mic (something with a rolled-off high-frequency response) or a dynamic mic might work better, especially if the tambourine is excessively bright.

Timbale

Timbale miking can change considerably depending on how the drum is being used. If the timbale is used in a Latin style, a cowbell will be attached to the drum that can easily overwhelm any mics aimed at the top of the instrument. If the music is salsa, the percussionist might opt to play on the side of the drum, which can best be captured by placing the mics under the drums.

Placement: Place a dynamic mic (a 57 or 421 works nicely) under each drum, about six to twelve inches away, angled at the head. To pick up the ambience and capture the full sound of the timbales, add an overhead mic about five feet above the center of the drums. Be sure to check the phase between the top and bottom mics.

Triangle

The triangle has a lot of transients, a lot of harmonics, and a lot of high-frequency energy, which makes it one of the hardest instruments to record. You can really tell the differences between preamps as a result (some engineers use a triangle as a test before buying). Try several different preamps if you have them available to you to see which sounds best.

Placement: Place a small diaphragm condenser mic in *omni* at least three to four feet away, slightly above the triangle and aiming down. Move the mic back until any low-frequency harmonics or microphone distortion disappears.

> ### Tips and Tricks
>
> Make sure to engage the high-pass filter either on the mic, the DAW, or console in order to decrease the low harmonics and any unwanted low-frequency noise or rumble.

EQING PERCUSSION

Percussion can easily conflict with the drum kit, guitars, vocals, and strings in a race for frequency space, and while they're very important to a mix because of the musical motion they convey, care must be taken when EQing.

Bongos, Congas: the ring that bongos and congas sometimes have can be accentuated at 200Hz, while the slap comes at 5kHz.

Shakers, Triangles: add 6–8kHz for more presence, and engage the high-pass filter.

> ### Tips and Tricks
>
> There's not normally much energy below 500Hz to 1kHz, so using the HPF below this point won't affect the sound while cleaning up some unwanted artifacts and rumbles that may have been captured during recording.

CHAPTER FOURTEEN
FINAL DRUM SOUND CHECKLIST

L ike the foundation of a house, the drums are the foundation of a recording. With a strong foundation, you can build almost anything on it that you or your clients can imagine. A little effort and time spent miking the drums and getting the sound just right can result in a recording that sounds better than you would ever have imagined.

Remember, take risks, experiment, take notes on what works and what doesn't, be creative, and most of all, use your ears and have fun!

Here's a list of things to check if something just doesn't sound right. Remember that each situation is different and, ultimately, the sound depends upon the drums, the drummer, the room, the song, the arrangement, the signal chain, and even the other players. It's not unusual to have at least one of these things out of your control.

- *Are the mics acoustically in phase?* Make sure that tom mics and room mics are parallel to each other. Make sure that any underneath mics are at a 90° angle to the top mics.
- *Are the mics electronically in phase?* Check that any bottom mics have the phase reversed. Make sure that all the mic cables are wired the same by doing a phase check.
- *Are the mics at the correct distance from the drum?* If they're too far away they'll pick up too much of the other drums. If they're too close the sound will be unbalanced with too much attack or ring.
- *Are the drum mics pointing at the center of the head?* Pointing at the center of the drum will give you the best balance of attack and fullness.
- *Are the cymbal mics pointed at the bell?* If the mic is pointed at the edge of the cymbal, you might hear more air "swishing" than cymbal tone.

- *Is the hi-hat mic pointed at the middle of the hat?* Too much towards the bell will make the sound thicker and duller. Too much towards the edge will make the sound thinner and can pick up more air noise.

- *Are the room mics parallel?* If you're using two room mics instead of a stereo mic to mike the room, make sure that the mics are on the same plane and are exactly parallel to each other. Also, make sure that they're on the very edge of the kit, looking at the outside edge of the cymbals.

- *Does the balance of the mix sound the same as when you're standing in front of the drums?* This is your reference point and what you should be trying to match. You can embellish the sound after you've achieved this.

These are not hard-and-fast rules, just a starting place. If you try something that's different from what you've read and it sounds good, it *is* good!

INTERVIEWS

BERNIE DRESEL

Like many session drummers in L.A., Bernie Dresel is noted for his ability to not only play any musical style, but being able to step in to play orchestral percussion or groove hand percussion as well. Widely recognized for his fifteen years with The Brian Setzer Orchestra, Bernie now does a variety of studio work that goes anywhere from the television shows like *The Simpsons* and *Family Guy*, to feature films, to the Blues-Rock of Carl Verheyen to the big band sound of Gordon Goodwin's Big Phat Band to R&B icons like Chaka Khan and Patti LaBelle.

Can you take us through your kit? Do you usually use the same kit in recording as live?
When I was touring with Brian Setzer, the kit evolved to be two 24"x14" bass drums with heads on the front and no hole and an external muffler on the beater side because we were doing a '40s big band sound, a 9"x13" rack, 16"x16" floor, and an 18"x16" floor. I even used calf-skin heads on the snare drum and tom batter side.

Originally, I had the standard DW setup of 10", 12", 14", and 16" with either Remo-coated Ambassadors or coated Emperors, but it was just too modern of a sound. We were trying to get that old tribal '40s [Gene] Krupa sound, and those were the sizes of the day back then. The calfskin heads gave it less of a pitch and made it much more "thuddy" and tribal. That was the kit seen by a lot of people since 1998. There's a lot of stuff on YouTube from a Christmas show and a show that we did in Japan in 2000, and that's the kit you'll see me playing.

In the studio for doing television shows like *The Simpsons*, *JAG*, *Family Guy*, or *American Dad*, I'd be using my basic studio kit. It's not a double bass drum kit, but I do set up a double bass drum pedal.

I generally have a 22"x16" kick, an 8"x12" high tom, and 14"x14" and 16"x16" floors. I use smaller, tighter drums for the studio, but that's what I would use to go out and play with most bands live, too. The oversize drums that I used with Brian [were] only for that period sound of the '40s.

I can make music with whatever is in front of me, but the idea was to duplicate the sound that they had back then, again with only a 14" depth and not 16" or 18", as is common now. I experimented with a 26", but the 24" was big enough to be a little tighter and not so boomy. Still, these bass drums were booming. I was playing "four on the floor" and they were easily heard, not like a Buddy Rich or bebop thing where every beat is "feathered" and you feel it instead of hearing it. I tried a calf head on the bass drums but it would rip too often with a plastic beater.

We would break down to a trio in the middle of the set and just do rockabilly songs where I would go out front with a cocktail kit that DW made for me with like a big 16"x24" tube where the bass drum beater would come up from the bottom. It's like a huge floor tom with a beater on the bottom and you can play the top of it like a floor tom with a sidecar snare and a cymbal attached. It was really bare bones. I could've gone out front and played a full kit but we were trying for a different sound here too.

Were you playing standing up?
Yes, exactly.

For basic studio stuff, I have a hole in the front head. I'm definitely a coated guy for the snare and the bass drum. I like the extra attack that the Remo-coated head brings. My thought is that an engineer can always dial out the top end if he wants, but if it's not there to begin with it's hard to add.

Generally I use Emperors on the toms and the bass drum with Emperor Ambassadors on the snare. Sometimes I'll go to coated Ambassadors on the toms, too, if it's more of a jazzy kind of thing, but session to session you don't know what's going to happen so most of the time I'll use Emperors on it. Some of that's for durability's sake, too, so you don't have to replace one halfway through the session.

How many snares do you usually bring to a session?
Here's the reality of today, at least with the stuff that I do. There are always budget considerations, so I generally bring six. I could bring

thirty snares but then the cartage bill goes up and, to be honest, you're usually way covered with the six snares because no one is ever asking, "What else you got?" past that.

I bring three different sizes of wood and three different sizes of metal drums. That's not including if I go to do an orchestral date, where I'd bring about eight different orchestral snares.

What's your collection like? Do you have a lot of drums?

Yeah, I guess I do, but it all boils down to, what are you going to send to a session? You have to send something that's pretty versatile and that's my DW kit. I have Radio King kits from the '40s with 24" and 26" bass drums, I have a Gretsch kit from 1947, a Leedy from the '40s, four DW kits, and a fifth DW kit that I took the bottom heads off for orchestral toms. If someone asked for a '70s sound, I have it ready to go.

That's not including all the different snares that I have. I even forget all them. I have some Radio Kings, Black Beauty's, a lot of cool Rogers stuff, Camco, a little bit of everything. I have six Johnny Craviotto Lake Superior snare drums. I love those snare drums. They found the wood at the bottom of Lake Superior, where it was underwater for about a hundred years after the logs sank. The trees were actually old growth from the 1300s, so between the wood and Johnny's construction they sound special and amazing. That's a newer drum, but it's old, old wood.

Generally when I buy vintage drums I don't buy something that's a collectable item. I try to get something that might have different rims on it, or was messed up cosmetically, or the edges have been redone by Johnny Craviotto, or something like that. These are usually worth less because the vintage market is based on originality or "mint condition." I don't want mint condition. I just want something to sound good. I must say that I have so much stuff now that I feel that I don't have to keep collecting at this point.

What did you use before DW?

I've been with DW since 1987. I had a Yamaha Recording Custom birch kit that was all the rage in the '80s, but I got tired of the sound of birch. I like maple shells.

How about tuning your drums? Do you tune to intervals? Do you have a particular method for tuning?

There're a lot of different theories about how a drum should sound, but the one that works best for me is when the top head is not exactly the same pitch as the bottom. The top head I tune about a minor third above the bottom head when you're just barely tapping it right on the edge, near the lug. Now it doesn't always stay right there because the head might loosen a bit when you're bashing on it, or the lugs might slip a little bit, but even if it drops a little to a second or a minor second, it's still tuned above the bottom head.

Are you tuning the bottom head to the resonant frequency of the drum?

You mean like when you have both heads off and you hit your fist on the inside of the shell to hear it ring? DW actually writes that pitch in their shell to be sure that all the drums are timbre matched so that you get a different pitch on each shell and they're not too close together. I'm not really sure how helpful that is as I've found that I usually don't tune to that pitch.

Really, the biggest thing is that you don't over-tighten and choke the drum or make it too loose because then it's a rather flat sound. I just try to get it within the sweet spot of a major third or so where you have some play yet it sounds good. Now if you were going to tune it up high like for a bebop session, then you'd want it a little choked.

What I try to do between my three toms, the 12", 14", and 16", is to have them maybe a fourth apart in pitch and that way you don't get an octave between the highest tom and the lowest, and they sound musical together. You could do fifths, but then you'd have a ninth off the top tom and it just seems too far away in pitch. Now if you have a lot of toms then maybe tuning them a major third apart could work, but with three toms I think a fourth is good because all three are tuned within the same octave and a fifth is too much because then they're not.

Again, when you hit the drum it starts to change, so you just try to keep it in check over the course of a song or a gig, realizing that it's never going to be perfect. The old days where you'd spend two days getting drum sounds actually seems ridiculous now, since after the third hour of getting sounds you'll hear, "OK, let's change the heads" (laughs).

Today it might take fifteen minutes or a half hour or even three minutes to get a drum sound. Before you know it you hear, "Okay, we're ready. Go!" There are some pretty good sounding drum kits now, and the engineers are hired for their drum sounds and speed because everyone is so budget conscious.

What drum do you start with when you're tuning your kit?

I don't think it matters. You can start at the top, you can start at the bottom, you can start in the middle. I tend to go top down, but just the other day I started with the low one. You just start to get a feeling for how many turns are needed when you're tightening the head. You get a feel for the right tension.

I don't think it's good to tune the snare drum on the snare stand. It's better on a table or floor so it's laying flat. You make sure you get your head on flat if you have to change one, then tighten each lug so that it's barely touching the rim, then just finger tighten the lugs (crisscrossing as you go) so you make sure that you don't over-tighten one, then you can start using the drum key. If you had eight arms so you could tighten all the lugs at the same time, that would be the best thing, but of course that's not possible.

Do you ever adjust the tuning of your drums to the song?

No, not the toms. Maybe the snare. It's not like you're tuning it to the pitch of the song because once you starting hitting it, it's going to change a little, so being exactly in tune isn't going to happen anyway. I feel that's being pretty anal about things, and the result is really not worth the effort because you're not getting a pitch out of the drum per se. You just want the drum to sound good.

I've had engineers and producers say, "I think your snare dropped a little," or "I think your snare is tuned too low. Bring it up in pitch a bit," or "The snare's sitting too tight," so you make those adjustments so it fits the songs. Sometimes you have to change snares from tune to tune, but within an album you don't change toms out. For as much as you're hitting them, it's not that drastic a thing because, after all, they sound like toms (laughs). The snare is a little more particular tune to tune, but then again, I've used one snare on every tune on an album and that works fine too, but it varies from project to project.

Now when I do *Family Guy*, I'll put up a snare drum and they'll say, "Okay, let's go." They figure that I'm going to pick the right thing musically for it. I'll usually use either a five inch or a four inch [depth]. I figure that snare size is something like skirt length. At one point everyone was going for that deep dish snare sound and then it changed to piccolo snares. It seems that everyone wants whatever everyone else is using at the time. Musically, I think that a lot of things can work; it just depends upon what the producer is going for, or what you happen to pull out of the case that day.

What do you want in the headphone mix when you're recording?

What you really want as a drummer is separate from what other people want. I think that there should be a rule that if there's a wall between you and another player, you need a different headphone mix. That means that I already hear plenty of drums in the room, but the other players can't hear drums at all.

If a bunch of horn guys are in the same room together, they can probably deal with the same mix, but they can't hear the drums on the other side of the wall or they can't hear the piano that's baffled off. The system where you dial in your own monitor mix (Aviom or Hearback) is the greatest thing because then you can just mix it on the fly or from tune to tune. If one of your bandmates is having some time problems, you might want to turn him down. In the case of the vocalist, you want to hear what's going on but you don't want it to get in the way of some of the groove things that you're playing.

I also want enough click, maybe more than the other players. Since the drums are such a "clicky" instrument already, you need more click than the other players. I do not want a cowbell or a side-stick as a click. I don't want a musical sound because it affects what I think is happening musically. I want a non-musical sound that's really short.

As far as headphones, I started experimenting with these sound-isolating Shures [SCL5s]. I liked those a lot because I didn't hear as much drums because that's what usually covers up the click more than anything. Usually I just use whatever phones are available as long as they're loud enough. Generally the studios I'm at all have good headphones, so I'm not particular in that regard.

Are there any particular mics that you like on your drums?

I thought for a while that I liked 421s on the toms because it seemed to make the toms sound fuller. A lot of times AKG 414s sound great, especially if you're playing jazz or brushes because they have a little more crispness. A lot of times when we're doing television I see engineers use the Neumann TLM-170s as overheads if they're going for a natural sound. They capture a great drum sound just from the overheads. They have them at Fox and Warner Bros. A lot of time, 414s are used as overheads if they're going for a rock sound. I always see a 57 on the snare.

Some guys want a mic underneath the snare and other guys don't need it and get the snappiness another way. It goes back and forth between an old 57 and a 451 on the bottom. I see all sorts of different things on the bass drum. Sometimes I'll see as many as three mics on the bass drum with something like a Neumann FET 47 way out in front.

The reason why I know more about mics now is because I now have my own home studio. I only record drums, although I might be able to do bass, too. People from Japan and Europe—or even five miles away—can get drum tracks from me over the Internet. That way you can save on the cartage and the general expense of booking a studio. The costs are cut quite a bit because I can schedule it in between my other sessions.

People still want me to play sessions because they still want everyone playing at once, whether it's an orchestra or just a rhythm section, so that's not going to go away, but now I can do a lot of budget things that I couldn't do before.

What are you using for cymbals?

I'm a Zildjian guy since 1986. I was a Zidjian guy as a kid, then when I first moved to L.A., I got a gig with the singing group The Lettermen. Zildjian wouldn't give me an endorsement at the time because The Lettermen weren't that big anymore, but Sabian did, so I was with Sabian for a second until I got the gig with Maynard Ferguson in 1986. They asked if I had a cymbal endorsement and I told them I was with Sabian, to which they replied, "Well, you're with Zildjian now."

It turns out that Armand Zildjian and Maynard were such great buddies that every drummer in his band had to play Zildjian, so suddenly I was back with who I wanted to be with anyway, and I've been with them ever since.

What sticks do you use?

Generally, I think you need a couple of types of sticks, not just one in your arsenal. If you're doing a wide range of stuff you need something that's softer with not as much weight when you need to be daintier, like in a jazz trio.

On a live gig where you need to play soft yet strong you need a thicker, beefier stick. When I played with The Brian Setzer Orchestra, I developed a Regal tip model called "The Bernie Dresel" model that was kind of a thicker bead with a little more length, a little more weight, and a little more throw that gets you more power and volume from the stick, so I think a couple of different kinds of sticks are appropriate to have.

Any advice for a young recording drummer?

I teach at UNLV [University of Nevada, Las Vegas] and give private lessons as well, so I'm really into the teaching process. I have advice for drummers whether they're recording or not, since it's not a matter of if the red light is on because someone is always listening anyway. A lot of drummers miss the boat because they're not concerned with playing time and playing simple basic beats and being able to clone that beat over and over again like a drum machine, but with soul. A lot of drummers are into the flash and constantly looking for stuff to play and where they put the kitchen sink into every tune.

I heard a story once where Miles Davis told someone, "When you think you want to play something, don't." That story is kinda funny, but it's also true. Don't try to be always playing something. Lay back, play the groove, and wait for your spot. They won't happen as often as you think.

A lot of times drummers try to play too much, and I'm not talking stylistically, either. Whether you're a fusion drummer or a groove drummer, a lot of young drummers are looking to play too much, too often. If you have amazing chops, wait for that right moment to use them. It will mean a lot more.

You want to be playing with a metronome, loops, and sequenced tracks as much as possible, and also playing without them. The last time I went to the NAMM [National Association of Music Merchants] show, I took a picture of one booth because there were people in every booth but this one. It was the metronome booth and it was empty. I thought to myself, "Ain't that the truth. Sometimes that's the last thing that people want to think about."

It's pretty cliché, but that's what keeps me working and what people want from a drummer. It's a support instrument and they want time, groove, and musicality from the drums. The rest is gravy.

As far as business, if you're looking to get into session work as a drummer, you can't do it. You just have to play a lot of gigs and wait for the time where you get that opportunity.

JOHNNY "VATOS" HERNANDEZ

During the '80s and the early '90s, Oingo Boingo was just about as big as a band could get in Southern California. Having parlayed their local buzz to major label record deals that produced several hits ("Only a Lad," "Dead Man's Party," "Weird Science") and movie appearances, the band called it quits in 1995. A member of Boingo for seventeen years, Johnny "Vatos" Hernandez, while best known as the rhythmic heart of Oingo Boingo, has gone on to use his widely diverse background to play on a variety of movies, television shows (*Battlestar Galactica*) and commercials (Tostitos, Honda, Kia, Chrysler) as well as a wide range of musical and orchestral gigs in all sorts of styles.

Give us a little of your background.
I went through all of my musical growing up in L.A., like doing pit shows, plays, and playing with the L.A. Junior Symphony during the '60s. During the '70s, I was on all the rock television shows, like *Midnight Special* and *Don Kirshner's Rock Concert*, when I played with Helen Reddy since she used to host them. We even got to play the *Johnny Carson Show* a couple of times when she [guest-]hosted that. Playing with Doc Severinsen's big band was really, really fun and is one of my career highlights.

In the '80s, I realized that there was a lot of rhythm section work available around town. I always wanted to be a studio player, and I was already leaning in that direction since I was playing all sorts of different styles. I happened to do a movie for Danny Elfman and Steve Bartek called *The Forbidden Zone*. Steve and I already knew each other since we had worked together with Don Ellis's big band and a few other things. Later on they heard me playing live and asked me to join The Mystic Knights of the Oingo Boingo, which then became Oingo Boingo. I did that for seventeen years and we did twelve albums and a few movies.

After that broke up, I went on the road with Tito and the Tarantula (they were in that movie *From Dusk Till Dawn*). I started working with Tito doing a TV show here in town called *Culture Clash* and I played with him for six or seven years until 9/11. We were doing our third European album and ready to go back with a lot of MTV coverage when the war started. I knew I probably couldn't get back into the country if I voiced my opinion about the war and George Bush, so I quit the band and stopped traveling. Now I play on jingles, on movies, and anything else that comes along.

I've known [this book's co-author] Dennis [Moody] since the '80s. We come from the same background as far as letting instruments sound the way they sound. You know, keep all the blue notes and all the funk, and all that stuff. We have the same kind of ears. I always appreciated his ability to not only work in a studio, but also in a live situation, which most studio guys don't have a clue about.

You had a trio that I used to love to watch.
It was a trio called Food for Feet. I loved that band. It was a project John [bass player John Avila] and I were working on before he was in Oingo Boingo. When Boingo went to audition bass players, I said, "I know this guy who can sing like a bird and play his ass off. Even though he doesn't fit right now, he's a chameleon and he'll take this band to another place." Well, we spent a lot of time auditioning everybody in town and John ended up getting the gig anyway (laughs), so that was our side project when Boingo wasn't playing. We would get into a van and go across the United States. We were wild, like three tornadoes.

What's your kit like? Do you use the same gear live as in the studio?
No, I'm always changing it up. I change it from ensemble to ensemble. With Boingo, we'd do two-and-a-half- or three-hour shows and they were all different styles, so I would have little changes here and there, like a bashing marching snare, or rototoms, or even a lot of extra toms.

Today when I'm in the studio the kit I use is pretty basic. For the most part if I'm doing jingles or a show, it's basically a four-piece kit. When I'm using my spectacular Johnny Vatos kit, it's 10", 12", 14", 16", and 18" tom-toms, a 12"x15" marching snare, a 13" piccolo snare, and a main 6"x14" inch snare. I usually use about three snares and a rototom.

Tell me about your studio kit.
I've been endorsed by DW [Drum Workshop, Inc.] for a long time. In fact, I was one of the very first guys endorsed by them. When Boingo went into the studio to do our first album in 1980, the Record Plant had this famous room that had marble floors and glass walls. You could hear every screw and rivet in the drums, so DW sent over a set of wood drums and I've been playing them ever since.

If I'm recording a TV commercial, generally I'll take a 16"x22" bass drum, an 8"x12" tom and a 14"x16" floor. I've put bass drum bearing edges on all the tom-toms, so they sound really fat and round and low. They don't necessarily carry well in a live situation, but for close miking in the studio they sit really well in a TV track.

If I'm doing a movie, I have a 24"x16" and a 24"x18" bass drum that I can switch to, depending on how much I want the subs [sub-woofers] to light up. When I had these bass drums made, I had them with the subs in the studio in mind.

The 18"x22" will hit the top end of the subs and the 16"x24" will hit both ends, so it's pretty hard to mix it out. What happens with anything larger, like with a 26" bass drum (which I've used only as a resonator) is that it'll fall off the bottom end of the track and get kind of lost. I have some old 1906 marching drums that I've had recut that I'll use as resonators for certain types of music, like we did with Tito and the Tarantula on an album called *Little Bitch*.

What are the shells made out of?

I tend to lean towards maple shells because I like the instant attack I get with them. DW made me a prototype oak set, but they decided that it would be too expensive to manufacture. I still have the set, though (laughs). I used the oak set on some of the *Battlestar Galactica* soundtracks that I played on. I really like them, especially in a track with a lot of percussion. They seem to have a nice but different kind of timbre.

By the time I got them I wasn't playing in Boingo much, so the budgets weren't enough for me to bring a big set most of the time. With Boingo I would bring as much as I could. I'd bring twenty different snare drums and six different bass drums, and I would make sure that I had just the right thing that would work best with each one of the tracks.

How many snare drums do you usually bring to a session now?

To a normal session I try to bring at least six. I'll bring a piccolo snare, a 4"x14", a 6" and a 5"x14", and a couple of wooden drums. The piccolos that I have are kind of regular 4.5"x14", but I have this one little Keplinger snare that I use once in a while. That's the general array of drums that I bring for jingles and soundtracks, but if I have an album project, I have thirty-five or forty different snare drums that I can bring.

Would you tailor the type of kit that you bring to the type of music that you'll be playing on?

Yeah, I always do.

What cymbals are you using?

I'm also a cymbal geek. I joined the Sabian Company in the early '80s and I'm always trying new cymbals that they come up with. I have all different kinds of hi-hat combinations. I like to mix and match the hi-hats a lot. I've never been able to play a standard set of hi-hats because I have to make sure that the spread is far enough apart and that they're going to blend with the rest of the cymbals. If I'm playing a bash ride, do I want the hats to be a little bit more raw and open or do I want them real tight, or do they have to blend with something like a twelve-string? It's all those little anal-retentive things that I've had the pleasure of enjoying (laughs).

What heads do you use?

I really like the Powerstroke 3 on the bass drum. Generally I'll use clear heads on all the bottoms, and then the tops vary. They're either white heads, or for my jazz kit and the kit that I use for acoustic music—like big band, where you can't play that loud—I have some of those Fiberskyn heads that look almost like calf heads, which I really love. You can tune them up high and they're real dark and they have a real skin-warm feel to them. I go between those for any acoustic music to clear heads for rock and pop stuff and sometimes the white heads, depending upon what era of rock or pop that I'll be playing.

Since you tune to the resonance of the shell, does that then determine your selection of tom sizes? In other words, do you go for something like an interval of a fourth or a third between the toms, or is it just whatever sounds good to your ear?

I'm a real stickler about tuning. I try to tune the drum as close as I can to the shell resonance. Fortunately, all my drums are timbre-matched, so the pitches don't get in the way of each other. I tap the side of the shell to see how it will sound in the room, then I tune it accordingly so that the drum is working at its maximum value in relation to the room. I do that everywhere I go, whether it's a ballroom or a wedding or Studio D at Village Recorders or Conway [famous Hollywood recording studios], or The House of Blues or the Gibson Amphitheater. I always tune the drums for the room.

My idea of a good-sounding drum is when you can just throw a mic in front of it and it works without any EQ or processing, which engineers love. That means there's less noise and distortion and the drum sounds bigger.

Do you tune for each song when you're doing a session? Do you tune to the key of the song?

No, but if I'm doing a project where we have all the time in the world, then I might. Usually we're on a budget where we have to do a lot of songs relatively quickly, so I'll just leave the same drums and tuning up and if one gets in the way tone-wise or is too close to the fundamental, then I won't use it.

When you tune your drums, which one do you start with?

I usually start with the kick drum, then go up to the floor tom to make sure that the kick doesn't set off the floor tom when I'm playing. I'll get those two pitches, and then that becomes the fundamental basic pitch reference for everything else. Then I work on the snare drum to get it sounding right against the bass drum. I'll determine whether I want them to sound like one unit or separate. I always try to make it separate although there are gut-bucket ways when you're playing funk where you tune down a 7"x14" snare where it rumbles along with the bass drum. I don't do that, though. I go for the separation.

Are there certain mics that complement your drums?

I really don't have any preferences. That's always up to the engineer because even 57s on the toms can sound okay with the right engineer. What I don't like are the mics that are hyped so that they supposedly sound good with drums. It's like Syndrums or something, where the manufacturers always talk down to drummers. "Oh, they like a lot of highs on their instrument," and you plug them in and the engineer goes, "What the ... is this?" That's why voicing and tuning the drums themselves is better than having a super-hyped mic.

What do you like in a phone mix?

Generally I like kick drum, a little bit of snare and hi-hat, a lot of click, and a basic mix of everything else. I don't need a lot of drums. I'd rather play with one earphone off my head and hear the drums naturally.

Would you rather hear a melodic click or an electronic one?

I begrudgingly use an electronic click, but I'd rather have a melodic one because they're really fun and easy to play to. If I had my choice I'd use a high go-go bell and a low go-go bell and then a side-stick for in-between (sings a rhythm), that way you always know where 1 and 3 and 2 and 4 are.

Do you ever use someone like the Drum Doctors to tune your drums?

I really like the Drum Doctor [Ross Garfield]. He's a cool guy, but only a couple of guys have ever come close to the tuning that I like, so I would rather do it myself because I'm so hyper-sensitive to hitting a drum and have another one ring. All that crosstalk crap has got to go.

The drum has got to have a lot of clarity and a lot of dynamic range. You have to hear both the stick and the roundness of the drum when you whack it, and that requires some sensitive tuning. It drives me insane sometimes. I've gone in and played house kits and I just have to close my eyes and pretend they sound great. It can be really annoying but I'll do it because I'm a musical prostitute (laughs).

Do you have any advice for someone who's just starting to record?

If it's the first time they've been in the studio, they have to learn the importance of *being* in the studio. If they say show up at four o'clock to start recording, they have to be there at three to set up. That's my first piece of advice—show up an hour ahead of when you're supposed to be there so you can make sure that you get the drums set up and tuned and ready to go.

Number two—practice playing with a metronome or rhythm machine and record yourself. Get a little recording device and make sure that you can play the feel and move the drums around against a click.

What happens is that you want to lay a click down because you might want to go back and overdub some stuff later. The engineer also wants to set delay and reverb times, so he needs the click, too. You might want to do all sort of technical things later and if you have tracks that push and pull it's never going to happen, so it's better to have two or three takes at the same tempo with all of your downbeats and fills locking in.

RICKY LAWSON

It just might be easier to say who Ricky Lawson hasn't played with rather than who he has. Unfortunately, Ricky passed away before the latest version of this book was published, but his interview is still as valuable as ever.

Having performed with Quincy Jones, the Brothers Johnson, Phil Collins, Steely Dan, Eric Clapton, Babyface, Lionel Ritchie, Anita Baker (*Rapture*), Whitney Houston ("I Will Always Love You") and as musical director for Michael Jackson. Ricky was also the original drummer for Yellowjackets, where he won best R&B Instrumental Grammy in 1987 ("And You Know That," the first track from the album *Shades*).

There's obviously a reason why these musical giants had him on a first-call basis and that's because not only was he massively talented, but exceedingly humble and helpful to others as well.

Can you describe your kit? Do you take a different kit on the road than you use in the studio?

I've been with the Pearl [Musical Instrument] Company for a while now and use a Pearl Studio Master kit with maple shells. I use a different kit on the road from the studio because the studio is such a detailed environment and everything has to be precise, since it's always under a microscope.

On the road things don't need to be so precise, so I take a different kit. With the economy being what it is these days, we can't always afford to take equipment with us on the road, so we get backline companies to supply us with equipment. I just order what I have at home and they supply it for me.

How do the kits differ?

They differ only because of the wear and tear on the road. You set it up, tear it down. Set it up, tear it down. Now that I'm blessed enough to have my own facility, I can set my gear up and leave it and it's always ready to go.

What size are your drums?

I generally use five toms in the studio—8"x8", 10"x10", 12"x12", 14"x14", and a 16" over on my hi-hat side. The bass drum is usually 22"x16". I'll use a host of different snare drums, depending upon what you're going for. For a hip-hop or R&B kind of vibe I'll use a snare that's 14"x6" or 6.5", so I have something that's reasonably deep.

Sometimes for something that's a little on the pop side, I may use a 14"x4.5" piccolo snare or maybe even a 13" snare, which has become very popular because it has more weight to it but still has the snap because of the smaller diameter. I've used snare drums as small as 10" in diameter and maybe 5.5" deep for jazz projects and hip-hop projects.

Usually I enjoy the wood snares better because they have a tendency to sound a little warmer than the metal snare drums, but it's all a combination of drum heads, the microphones, the processing, and the engineer to make things sound good. You can have a $10,000 drum kit and he can make things sound like cracker boxes, and you can have cracker boxes and he can make it sound like a $10,000 kit. There are a lot of little factors that make a difference, and what we try to do is cut down as many as possible or turn them to our advantage.

That means I have my own kit tuned the way I like it, with the heads that I like and with the kind of microphones and the kind of engineer that I know can capture it, because a lot of engineers cannot capture what a real acoustic drum set sounds like.

What heads are you using?
I use Remo heads. I like a Control Sound coated snare head with the dot up under the bottom because it's coated so that I can use brushes on it if I have to. On the toms I use Emperor heads on the tops and Ambassadors on the bottom.

Sometimes I go with the clear head because it's a bit more metallic and cracking, but if I'm doing something that's more jazzy, I'll use a coated Emperor head. I just kind of move the combination of drum heads around to get different things. If I want a heavier sound, I'll use a thicker head. If I want it brighter with more attack, I'll use a thinner head. I usually don't go any thinner than an Ambassador and I usually don't go any thicker than an Emperor. I go with Remo because they make more combinations than anybody out there and their stuff is more consistent.

For the bass drum I use a Power Stroke, which is not as thick as a Pinstripe but not as thin as an Ambassador. I try to use a 16" bass drum because that'll give me a little more weight and body to the kick drum.

It's so funny, when I played with Phil Collins, he used a 20" bass drum but it was 16" deep. He has to use a smaller bass drum in order to get the toms physically in there because he has those big giant toms. Yet if you listen to "In the Air Tonight," that 20" bass drum sounds a lot bigger because it's all in the engineering.

What mics do you like to use on your kit?
I always use Shure mics because they're consistent and always work. When I toured with Steely Dan those were the mics that we used. We used the KSMs, the VP-88, and the Beta 52. If a guy pulls these mics out I know it's usually going to be great. About 95 percent of the time they use an SM-57 on the snare drum. I've seen some teeny, tiny mics where the guy got a killer sound and I've had a session where the guy used $30,000 worth of mics on the drums and it sounded like $500 worth.

I'm telling you that the sound is in the engineering and the studio environment. It's not really what I like to see on the drums, it's who I see engineering because you can get a cat that doesn't know what he's doing and it can be a nightmare. Back in the day, they might have only used three or four mics, tops, but if a guy knew what he was doing, he got a killer drum sound. It's the engineering factor that plays such a big part in the situation.

Do you tune your drums to intervals?
What I try to do is to tune to where the drum sounds good. You can take a drum and you can tune it out of the range of what it likes to be in, so I just try to find the sweet spot for that drum with the combination of heads that I'm using. I like the top head a little bit tighter and then I use the bottom head just to bring in some tone.

For more of a big tom kind of vibe I've been using some open bottom toms that don't have a bottom head and that's pretty interesting, too. On some of the George Duke projects that I've done, I didn't use a bottom head on my first four toms. It's a little bit more of a caveman kind of tom sound. I kind of jump back and forth, depending upon what is needed.

How many snare drums do you bring to a session?
Usually five or six. At my studio I have about eight that I'll regularly choose from. You'd be surprised, different drums bring out different spirit in the music. I used some snare drums that were as big as a coffee can and it sounded huge just by backing the mic away and capturing more of the sound with the overhead mics. If you play a fatter

drum you have to get in a little bit closer so it can capture that meat, that body of the drum.

I went through four snares on the last session that I did, not because they sounded bad but because the client wanted to blend my snare along with the electronic snare drum they had going on. We changed them until we found the right one because my job is to give them what they're looking for, and in this case, that's what they wanted.

Sometimes people think that a snare drum is going to sound a particular way because of the size of it, but it all depends on the tuning of the drum. I always tell them, "Hey, let me know what you need and I'll get you there," because that's my job, to get them exactly what they need.

Do you tailor the kit that you bring to the session to the type of music?
Yes, sir. If we're doing pop, I'll make sure that I have some big toms, and if we're doing jazz, the toms will be a little bit smaller so the sound isn't as bombastic. A lot of times I choose a kit that's pretty general that I can use it on just about anything. With the 8", 10", and 12" with 14" and 16" floor toms, I can do pretty much anything that's going down. I can play jazz, I can play funk, I can play pop, or I can play Gospel with that kit. Whatever is necessary.

At my studio I use four toms but I have the ability to add two more to that configuration, but I bring five toms to an outside session.

Do you tune your toms to intervals?
No, what I do is find the range of the drum and get the drum sounding good. If I get the drum sounding like what it's supposed to sound like, then I'm done. Maybe I'll add a little duct tape to take out some of the overtones, but other than that, I'm through.

Do you have a hole in your kick drum or do you take the front head off?
Sometimes I have to take the front head off, but generally I have a hole in it. That hole is usually anywhere from 8" to maybe 12".

What kind of cymbals do you use?
Right now I use the Paiste Signature line. I used it on the Steely Dan tour, the Phil Collins tour, all over the place. The hats are 13" heavies. You can play pretty much any style of music with those. I use a

17" crash, 16" crash, 20" dry ride, and a 20" China that I can use on straight ahead, Latin, jazz, or funk. The nice thing is that they stay brighter and clearer longer. I use a wood-tipped stick so they sound cleaner and makes it easy for me to do what I do.

What do you like to hear in the mix?

I like to hear the piano, a little bit of the bass, ambience on myself, and whatever the lead instrument is so I can get a feel for the melody to know how to approach my particular part. Gotta have the click, too.

Do you like a musical click or something mechanical?

Preferably a musical one, but I'm one of those kind of cats that can work with whatever. Give it to me more on the musical side, but if not, I'll use whatever you got. It can be an old lady clapping her hands—I'll take that and work with it. I've done sessions where the guys have had it together, which is great, and I've done sessions where the guys didn't have it together. The key is to get in and make it happen in the least amount of time.

I actually prefer to work at my place because it's already set up, it sounds really good, and we can work a lot more efficiently in that we can do more tracks in not a lot of time. On one session recently we cut nine tracks in seven hours because of the efficiency of the studio. The artist was losing his mind because he was used to getting maybe two tracks on a good day.

Is there a set of headphones that you like to use?

I like the Sony professional headphones. I like the way that they fit on my head. There's also an AKG set that I really like that sounds fantastic.

Any advice for someone just starting to record?

As far as advice, the first thing is to play good time. Secondly, you have to make it feel good. If you don't, you're going to get beat up from having to play it over and over again. I usually try to get stuff done in one or two takes. Hopefully I can get it done in one (laughs), but if not, two or three is not bad. But job one is to play good time.

Do you have any tricks to making things feel good?

No, man, I just listen to the music and I try to play it as if I wrote it. When you think like that you have a tendency to play it a lot differently than if you just got it cold. A lot of time we haven't heard the music or seen the artist before. That's the biggest drag. It's hard to get the music cold, figure it out, and then play it as if you've been playing it for years. Then you have to make it happen in the least amount of time on top of that. Usually a session is three and half hours and you've got to get it done in that time, and that's if you're by yourself [overdubbing drums].

Sometimes the other drag can be if you have other musicians involved because you may have to pull them into it as well, which adds another factor to what's going on, but if you have good guys, it's almost like a good basketball team. Once the music is counted off they know exactly where they're supposed to go and how to get there. They just come in and take everything to the next level, and that's a hit when you can do that.

What's the most magical gig you've ever done?
Michael Jackson's gig was the ultimate just because of the quality of the musicians and the dimension of the show. That was one of my best. Also, working for Walter Becker and Donald Fagen [the founders of Steely Dan]. Working with those guys you cannot help but kick booty. And, of course, the Yellowjackets, where having your own music be recognized and win a Grammy felt so good.

The thing is, the Yellowjackets were just a band playing music that we liked. It wasn't like, "Let's go out and change the world." We were just having fun and it really worked out. Now I hear that music somewhere every day.

BRIAN MACLEOD

Brian MacLeod has been one of the most in-demand session drummers in L.A. for quite some time now, and with good reason. Brian has the ability to make tracks feel not just pretty good, but awesomely great. Although he has plenty of chops, just listen to the groove in Sheryl Crow's breakthrough hit "All I Wanna Do" and you'll hear exactly what Brian is known for. And if you're a fan of the television shows *The Office* or *Dirty Sexy Money*, that's him playing on the theme song. Add to this, credits like Christina Aguilera, Madonna, Chris Isaac, John Hiatt, Tears for Fears, Jewel and many, many more, and you get the picture of just why the Brian MacLeod touch is so sought after.

But there's more to Brian than just drumming. As a member of the *Tuesday Night Music Club*, the 1993 album that shot Sheryl Crow to fame, he's been Crow's frequent songwriting collaborator in the years hence, helping pen (among many other songs) the ever-popular "Every Day Is a Winding Road," which seems to be used in a television commercial or movie soundtrack every year.

What's your kit like?

I switched from using my vintage gear to a custom DDrum kit. They've been around for a long time making drum triggers but this is kind of a new thing from them. I still love my old Gretsch and Ludwig kits, but DDrum made me a beautiful custom kit with a lot of additional pieces, like different-size kick drums.

They made me 20", 22", and 26" kicks because they all have specific sounds. The 20" is punchy for R&B, the 22" is good for modern rock and commercial stuff, and then the 26" is for that John Bonham thing with both heads on.

These are all 16" deep?

The 26" is 14" deep. The other two are 16" deep.

This drum kit is all maple and really sounds warm. It has wood hoops on all the toms and is kind of modeled after the old marching kits that Levon Helm (of The Band) used to play. I've been using it a lot as my starting place, but I'll use different gear for different projects. Sometimes I won't bring everything, but I generally like to have a lot of options so I'll bring a big arsenal.

I also like to have a lot of odd things, like toy snare drums, that

I've picked up along the way, which are great for making drum loops. I have a bunch of lo-fi trashy cymbals that I use sometimes when I don't want to go for a hi-tech sound, but I like to have a big array of available sounds to choose from that go from hi-tech to lo-tech.

I have this other drum that's really interesting called the "Trash Cat," which is like a tympani but it's made out of a trash can. I can use it like a floor tom or like a tympani. A lot of producers have really fallen in love with it.

It's nice to have odd, different things available. I interject them when the producer is looking for something special. It really takes a lot of teamwork with the producer as a session drummer. You have to go with the flow and not interrupt things, but at the same time, have something to bring to the table, if needed.

How many toms do you bring?

I generally play a 12"x8" and a 16"x14", but I also bring a 14"x14" floor tom if I need another one.

What kind of heads do you use?

I generally use Ambassador coated heads. I'm not afraid to tape up my kit if I need to get it to fit better with the song, though, because you have to tune your drums for the microphones. Sometimes the drum kit might not sound good in the room after you tune it, but it might sound amazing when you hear a playback. This can be very deceiving for young drummers especially. A young drummer might have his kit tuned so they sound just wonderful live, but you tune it differently for recording. Sometimes I'll use tons of duct tape. I'm not afraid to tape up drums or pad them down to get a nice tight sound if that's what the producer is looking for.

How do you tune your drums? Do you tune to an interval?

I'm not one of those guys who gets into interval tuning. I think that most drums have a sweet spot and that's what I try to find. It might not necessarily be an interval with another drum, although sometimes I will do that with the snare drum, especially if it's wide open for a real loud and cracking sound. Then I'll either tune it to the pitch of the song so it sits in there nicely, or just the opposite, where it's out of pitch with the song so it clanks a bit. Sometimes that means just detuning one lug of the snare to get a nice, loud *crack* out of it.

When you say the "sweet spot," do you mean the resonant frequency of the drum?

Yeah, that's what it is. I learned a lot about tuning from working with the Drum Doctor [Ross Garfield] for so many years, and John Good from DW [Drum World] taught me a lot about the sound that each shell has. Just naturally when you're playing with the drum you'll hit a spot where it feels really good.

Some of the older drums that have rounded bearing edges have kind of a deader sound, so it's harder to find the sweet spot. This drum kit that I have doesn't have the standard 45° edge like most new drums. It has a 30° edge, so it sounds more like older drums because that's the sound I really like. I'm having them build a mahogany kit for me because it's a warmer sound than maple. Some of my old Slingerland Radio King kits are mahogany and they just sound so warm, but the sweet spot you seem to instinctually find.

Like I was saying before, sometimes I'll hit a drum and it just doesn't sound good, but before I'll go and tune it I'll wait until the engineer tells me what he's hearing in the control room because the sound that you hear sitting behind the kit is so different from what the mics hear. Sometimes I'll think that the drum sound is amazing and the engineer or producer will go, "Man, that tom is a little ringy and high. Can you tune it down a bit?" I'll tune it down a bit and it will sound floppy to me and might not even physically feel right hitting it, but when I go back into the control room and listen to it, it just sounds huge and wonderful.

Tuning can be a bit of a mystery. It's very instinctual. There's no real math to it, as far as I know.

Do you use the Drum Doctor on sessions?

When the session budget is big, I like to use him. When the budget isn't big I have to do it myself. I've learned a lot by working with Ross for so many years so I can make it sound pretty good, but it's really nice to walk into a session and know that he's tuned it up and I can just show up and play. I don't like to get bogged down in the studio tuning drums. It can really slow down the session and I like to keep the pace of the session up and moving forward.

You mentioned the fact that you bring different drums to different types of sessions. How do you determine what to bring for something like a Chris Isaac session as compared to a movie or television gig?

Generally I try to get a heads-up from the producer or the producer's assistant as to what kind of song we're doing and what he wants it to sound like. Like, if he says they're doing something that's a retro-'70s Led Zeppelin–type of thing, then I know to bring my 26" kick and an old Radio King snare. If he says that it's a mid-tempo R&B kind of thing, then I'll know to bring my 20" or 22" kick. I try to get as much information from the producer before the session and find out as much about the artist, the specific band, and the direction of the music.

It sounds like you have a big drum collection.
Oh, yeah (laughs). I've got a huge collection parked at the Drum Doctors, and my garage is completely full with just a very small aisle down the middle. I'm constantly scouring Ebay for new weird things like plastic snare drums and odds and ends.

I like to have a lot of toys just to make sure that the recording is interesting. That's something I got from [well-known session drummer] Jim Keltner. Sometimes if he's in a session in the studio next to mine we go hang out together and we're like little kids, comparing our new, odd toys and instruments. He's always been a big help on that kind of stuff.

How many snares do you bring to a session?
I have two trunks that I generally bring that contain ten snare drums, plus I have an old vintage '70s Black Beauty that I hand-carry with me. That always stays at home with me and I bring it to work just like it was my brief case (laughs).

I've got some old '20s chrome-over-brass drums, and some big old mahogany drums that are great for that '70s sound. They have six lugs and round bearing edges so they tune down really low, and if you tape it up it gets a really fat sound that's great for ballads. I generally don't use a piccolo, but I have one in my arsenal. You have to make sure that you have everything because whatever it is that you don't bring to the session, that's what the producer will ask for, so I like to be prepared and have plenty of options.

Once again, that has to fit with the budget. If it's a full record, I try to bring as much stuff as I can and almost every day that I come in I'll bring even more stuff. If I hear something for a specific song, I'll dig around and maybe find something that I think will work if I bring it. It varies, but I generally have ten snare drums that represent a good spectrum from piccolos to big fat '70s sounds.

What do you use for cymbals?
I've been using Paiste Giant Beat cymbals, but I have so many old vintage Zildjians from the '50s and '60s, which I collect. I like to have a pair of 13", 14", and 15" hi-hats available at a session. The 13s are really tight and the 15s are really dark and warm.

I've noticed over the years that recording hi-hat can be really tricky. You might put a mic on it and never even use it because it's so loud, so I like to have some quiet hats around. I have these 15s that are quiet and nice sounding.

I generally use 17", 18", and 20" crashes and a couple of 20s and a couple of 22" rides. I also have one sizzle cymbal that I bring, although some engineers are allergic to them (laughs). The sizzle cymbal opens a whole floodgate of either people who love them or hate them, but I make sure that I have some with me at all times.

How about sticks?
I usually play 5As because they're such an all-around good stick, but sometimes I'll use different types. I'll use the Fatar Recording drumsticks that have a small bead on them, which I really like because then you can get a really good cymbal sound.

It's really amazing how a different bead can make the cymbal sound completely different when you're riding on a cymbal. If you use a round head you'll get a lot of attack. If you use a plastic head you'll get more attack. If you use a larger wood you can get more of a wash from the cymbal, so I definitely have a lot of different sticks and brushes and mallets too, because someone will always ask, "Can you do a cymbal swell?"

If you look in your stick bag and you don't have what they asked for, that's the part of being a session drummer where you have the most anxiety. It gets embarrassing if you have to tell them, "I can make some with some tissues and duct tape (laughs hard)." I like to make sure that my stick bag is loaded with hot-rods, brushes, different-sized sticks and mallets.

You don't do too much live work these days, do you?
No, I don't do much at all. It's so funny because since I've moved to L.A. I've played live maybe ten times in fifteen years. I don't really tour too much because I like to be available for sessions. The last big tour that I did was with Tears for Fears, but I had to come back and re-

establish myself with all the producers because I was gone for such a long period of time. Out of sight, out of mind, as they would say. Now if Nick Mason decides he doesn't want to play with Pink Floyd anymore, then that would be something I'd have to think about (laughs).

That begs the question, would your road kit be different than what you'd use in the studio?

Probably. I probably wouldn't use wood hoops and it would be tuned more open and live. I'd work with the front-of-house guy to dial in the kit. Then visually, I'd probably do something a bit different too. When I did the *Jay Leno Show* with Seal I used my clear acrylic DW kit because it just looks so good on TV. The lighting people just love it. So yeah, I'd use a different kit live because I'd go for the fashion (laughs). It's like wearing different ties with your suit.

What's so funny about the studio [is that] sometimes I'll just have such a mis-matched kit with like my red sparkle 14" Ludwig floor tom with my DW 26" kick and an old Gretsch 13" rack tom. They look like a disaster together, but sound great.

What are you looking for in the headphones when you record?

That's a great question. Generally it depends on how we're tracking. If I'm tracking with a bass player and we're doing overdubs to an existing track, I'll try to get a nice even level so it sounds like a record, with the vocals and the bass player just above the music. I want to hear the bass player so I can be sure to lock my kick drum with him.

If I'm tracking live I want whoever is the leader of the song to be above the track. Like, if the guitar player has written the song, he might be doing some important inflections that I need to hear. If it's a vocalist who has written the song and they're evoking some emotion that they really want, I'll make sure that is above everything else. I try to latch on to whatever the main instrument of the tracking date is, or what the biggest concern seems to be when laying down the basics.

I'll also have the click at an ungodly level, which can drive producers and engineers crazy, so I like to use closed headphones for that. I'm still looking for the perfect set of headphones because you don't want the click track leaking into the song. On Christina Aguilera's "Beautiful," you can hear a bit of the drum machine on her vocal track, but the vocal was so amazing that they just went with it. You have to be careful, especially on endings of songs. I try to get the engineer to cut the click off so that the cymbal sustain doesn't have any click bleed. I'll even punch in the ending of a song if they can't catch it at the right time.

What kind of a click sound do you like?
In the old days I used to be very specific about it. I used to like a cowbell or some sort of side-stick sound with a shaker doing 16ths or 8ths depending on the feel of the song. I have to say that's still my favorite click track, but I'm getting used to just the standard Protools click. I've adjusted over the years, but my preference still is the cowbell and shaker.

Do you any mic preferences?
Depending on the engineer and the producer, if they have a preference I'll go with what they want, but I gotta say I really love a FET-47 on the outside of the kick drum. That's one of my favorite mics. I like ribbon mics a lot for room and overheads. I like the Beyer M-160 ribbon on the hat. That warms it up a lot.

I did a session the other day where we used Sony C-37s on the toms (which haven't been made since the late '60s), and they sounded amazing. The producer said, "If you weren't the drummer on the session, I wouldn't put them up," because they're so fragile that you have to be afraid of hitting them. That was really quite a compliment. Then again, some people get great results from Sennheiser 421s.

I don't generally do top and bottom mics on the toms. I don't like too many mics on the drum kit unless the producer and engineer are really paying attention to the phase cancellation, but I have had good results with people who have done it that way. I walked into a session with a metal producer who shall remain nameless, and he had the kit miked up with what looked like forty microphones. I thought, This is ridiculous, but I played the track and it sounded amazing. Then sometimes I'll work with just three mics on the kit and it will sound great, too. Everybody has their own technique and I try to be flexible because most of the people that I work with are so high-end that I trust them to get my drums sounding the way they want them to sound.

Do you have any other advice for a young drummer just starting out?
Yeah, I'd say try to play to a click as much as you can so you can learn to play with it yet lose sight of it at the same time. You want the feel

of the click track to become like intuition, so it doesn't make you feel shackled to it.

Also, when you work with a producer, be as flexible as you can be. Don't be stubborn, and trust the people you work with. If the engineer or producer has a suggestion, trust their advice. If I work with a producer that wants me to play his old vintage kit, of course I'll play it because I think it's important to be flexible. Even if you show up with your gear, if he has his kit miked up and he knows what it sounds like, I'll generally do that. If they're not satisfied, then I'll use my drums.

Another thing, if you have any ideas, make the suggestion if the time is right because it's all about teamwork and you're on the team.

You mentioned before about (producer) Patrick Leonard inviting you to L.A. to record. Would you consider that your big break?
I think so because after we finished that record I was pretty much planning on moving back to the Bay Area, but Patrick said, "Hey Brian, if you lived in L.A. I would use you on the records I work on." Ironically the engineer/co-producer on that record was Bill Bottrell [who eventually went on to produce Sheryl Crow, Michael Jackson, and Shelby Lynn] and he said the same thing to me, so I had two top-of-the-line producers tell me that if I lived in L.A. they'd use me on their records. It became a no-brainer for me to run up to the Bay Area, pack my things in a U-Haul, and get my butt to L.A. It kind of expanded from there.

I had no delusions of moving to L.A. before those sessions. I was too content up in the Bay Area where I had a nice life teaching drums and playing live almost every night. It was wonderful, so I really didn't want to move to L.A. unless there was a good reason because I didn't just want to try to break in the way everyone seems to do it. It would have been too frustrating for me.

What's your favorite type of music to play?
It's an interesting spectrum. I love retro-funk, and I love old hard rock. I think that stems from my older brothers blasting The Beatles to Led Zeppelin in their bedrooms while my mom was out vacuuming the living room, listening to R&B. With my mom listening to Aretha Franklin and The Supremes and my brothers teaching me about rock 'n' roll, that's really how I got started. My brothers were guitar players and they needed a drummer, so they got me a drum kit. They were

trying to make me the first human drum machine at eight years old (laughs), but I just fell in love with it and became obsessed. I knew even at that age that's what I wanted to do. I used to stare at pictures of The Who and Led Zeppelin playing in the studio and go, "That's what I want to do. I want to work in studios."

What's the best gig you've ever had?

I would have to say being part of the *Tuesday Night Music Club*. As you know, we wrote and conceived what became Sheryl Crow's first album. It was awesome. We were all working in the studio and [producer] Bill Bottrell made sure that everybody participated to the point where sometimes I wasn't even playing drums. He'd make me play bass or something. It was kind of frightening, but fun at the same time.

It was one of the most incredible experiences in my life to participate in, not just as a drummer but as a musician and a lyricist. He really opened the door to all of us to push the envelope.

That whole period of time was really wonderful, but continuing to write songs with Sheryl Crow after that was really great, too. She's always been open to my ideas. It's great to have someone believe and trust in you like she has.

Also, I have to say that touring with Tears for Fears was really wonderful, too, because they had such great songs. Just playing those songs live was pretty awesome.

What kind of gig is the hardest for you?

The hardest gig is when the artist and/or the producer doesn't know what they want and they're not open to suggestions. That can be really difficult because even though they don't know what they want, they won't accept any help to find out what they may want.

I've done a couple of records like that where I'd pull my hair out because they just kept experimenting. "Let's try it reggae style," "No, let's try it as a waltz." They'd just keep going around in circles, but at the same time didn't want to hear your opinion or suggestion. "We just want to keep going around chopping the legs off the chair until there's no vibe left."

What are the most fun gigs?

Tracking live is so much fun when I play with musicians that I really connect with. I get a little of that live feel and edge, but it's in the studio, so it sounds good. It's musical communication and connection. I guess it goes back to looking at those records when I was a kid. To see The Beatles all set up in the studio with George Martin in the middle talking to them, I pine for those days (laughs).

Is there an aspect to recording that you don't like?
Yes, when they "drive past the money." If there's an amazing take that was done live and they say something like, "We don't like the ending to the song. Can we do another take?" When you feel like you've done something really wonderful and either the producer or the artist kinda just drives right past it and then beats the song into the ground and sucks the life out of it. Sometimes there's magic in takes that end up never getting used. That can be really frustrating. That's happened a lot, unfortunately.

I think that it's one of those things where you almost have to be playing to know when you've really nailed it. It's really hard to be on the other side of the glass and know when you've caught the magic. That's the trick of being a producer.
Exactly, and I've had to swallow my pride and play something faster or slower and it doesn't sound as good, but if they want it that way, you've just got to do it. This isn't my record after all, it's theirs.

Is there an aspect of drumming that you don't like?
Hauling my gear around (laughs). I think the day when I bought my convertible and could drive it to a session I felt like success. I thought, I don't have to drive a van around any more. I can just come in my Alfa Romero to this wonderful studio with these wonderful musicians with my drums already tuned to where I just walk in and play. I know that sounds [like I'm] spoiled, but at some point in any musician's life, that's a reward.

KELLII SCOTT

Kellii Scott has played drums with the alternative rock band Failure on and off for more than twenty years. In between he was a member of esteemed producer Lynda Perry's studio band and drummed on projects by Christina Aguilera, Pink, Faith Hill, Hole, Scissor Sisters, and many others. Kellii was on a short break in the middle of touring when this interview was conducted, as was about to head back out to Europe.

When you tour out of the country, do you take your own kit with you?
No, because I endorse Gretsch and Meinl cymbals, I call my guys there and they have a drum set and cymbals available for me ready to go. Next year we'll be doing a lot of fly dates so I'll do the same thing—just call the drum and cymbal companies and they'll arrange everything for me.

Do you bring a snare or anything with you?
I usually bring my secret weapon snare with me. It's this weird snare that I got off of Ebay about five or six years ago, and I haven't used anything else live since. I'll bring that, a stick bag, and usually a kick drum pedal.

What makes this particular snare so special?
Most of the touring I've done over the last few years calls for me to play more on the aggressive side. This particular snare weighs between thirty-four and thirty-seven pounds, so I can play it very softly or I can play it very hard and the drum never chokes. It's super explosive, and I really like the sound.

How does it record?
It records great. It's actually the only snare that I used during the recording of our last record. I brought a bunch of snare drums with me to the studio, but that one sounded so good that it never came off the drum set. I would retune it to the track so there weren't any weird overtones, and that actually made it sound like more than one snare drum.

What's your kit like these days?
For the Failure stuff it's pretty small; just a 13" rack, a 16" floor tom, and a 24" kick. The kick is kind of vintage in that it's 14"x24", so it's not as deep.

The reason why I picked the size of my drums is so I can get more out of them just by tuning them differently. Because the kick is so shallow, I can make it sound more like a 22" just by pitching it up a little bit, and I can make it sound like a 26" by pitching it down really low.

How do you tune it for touring?
I set it nice and flappy, almost like the heads are going to fall off. When I do that it tends to get a broader spectrum of sound with some real lows and some real highs.

Do you have a front head on?
Yes, I've got a double ply on each side and there's a hole in the front head. I use one of those homemade sub kick mics with the inverted NS10 speaker for some sub. I tune both heads pretty low, with very little padding inside of it.

Are they tuned the same?
No, the one on the kick side is a clear P3 (Remo Powerstroke 3), and the one on the outside is a coated P4 and it has our band logo on top of it.

How did you come up with this setup?
Some of it came from studio experience, and getting to that place where you know that you can tune a drum to where it's the way someone else wants it to sound. That really helped me develop my own particular voice where not only the sound of the drum resonates with me but the way it feels to play it. I want it to sound great but at the same time I want it to be comfortable to play. I don't want to have to exert myself or adjust my technique to play something, so I sort of go from there.

Depending on the drum, I don't always get it to where it's easiest to play but I try to keep that window as small as possible.

When you're in the studio, do you tune your own drums or bring a tuner in to do it?
I do all of it myself. I've always kind of known how I wanted the drums to sound but it wasn't until I worked for Linda Perry that I really figured it out.

Lynda had me not only playing all the drums on her records but doing all of the teching as well. That started with me spending weeks going through her massive drum collection and learning to tune them to where they sounded best based on their particular depth, wood type, and the heads I put on them. I think that's where I learned the most about the individual voices of drums.

Before that I would just grab any drum and tune it the way I wanted it to sound as opposed to tuning the drum the way it wants to sound. You kind of have to take all that information and put it together without having it mess with your technique and get it to where you're most comfortable playing. You have to find a small enough window where you feel comfortable and the drum sounds comfortable, if that makes any sense.

How about heads?

Over the years I haven't really changed that much. I've always liked clear heads on the kick drum and coated dot heads on the snare. Over time I've gotten a little bit thicker on my snare heads. I like them tuned somewhere in the middle to just above the middle in tightness. You tend to get a lot of weird overtones in that area, so I find that the thicker the head the less I have to struggle with those overtones.

I'm not a big fan of changing the heads all the time. I think it's kind of wasteful. There's definitely a sweet spot where a drum really starts to fall in love with the head that's on it and it sounds better when it's worn in a little bit. Because I tend to play hard, all of that dovetails together. I use all of that to determine what best suits my playing without having as many unwanted overtones as possible.

I used to use double-ply coated heads for the toms, which I still do, but I've switched to those Evans Onyx black ones. They're very easy to tune, they're pretty rich sounding, and again they're pretty thick so they don't have a lot of overtones to them, because I don't like to put muffling on drums at all.

Wow, that's unusual.

Yeah, those I can play pretty wide open with no muffling and there won't be a lot of crazy overtones. They're also super durable. I can leave them on for up to a week and a half sometimes. I change them at that time even though they still feel and sound good, but I play pretty hard.

That said, I have a series of snares that I only use in the studio and I never touch the heads on those because in the studio I play completely different than I do live. The heads have been on those for years and I'd never dream of changing them. Live, my job is to beat the vitality out of the drums, so I'm forced to change the heads more often.

Just to be clear, a new drum head always sounds great on a drum, but sometimes leaving a head on for a while really works as long as it's suited to the player. There are definitely multiple ways of looking at it. Personally, I'd much rather leave the drum head on for as long as possible.

I change my drum heads every week and a half or so when I'm playing live, but to this day I've never seen any extreme pitting, even though I play pretty hard. These black onyx heads are so durable.

What do you do with the old heads?
I either keep them around and save them for a rainy day, depending on my finances, or I'll sign them and give them away or put them at the merch booth to help pay for all the sticks and heads I bought during the tour. I never throw them away. Even if they're worth nothing to me, they're worth something to someone else.

Did you ever have a defining moment during your career that made you think of your career or playing differently?
My first band out here [in Los Angeles] that I recorded a record with had two drummers. There was me and John Molo, the drummer that eventually played with Bruce Hornsby and now plays with John Fogerty. At the time he was in his mid- to late-thirties and had been a pro drummer for a long time, and I was eighteen and young and scrappy. I had this energy, but I didn't know the first thing about what a drummer actually does besides show off.

I was fortunate in that Michael Beinhorn was producing the record and he recognized this in me. He pulled me aside and said, "You're competing for space on this record and you're going to get slaughtered if you continue to do what you do. You can take my advice and put in some work in the right direction or continue like you are."

He had the foresight to have one of the assistants put a drum set in a bungalow by the studio, and he asked me to sit up there with [ACDC's 1979 album] *Highway To Hell*. He said, "Spend the entire weekend playing this record, but understand what it is that makes this record and this drummer [Phil Rudd] so great."

He made me imagine that if there's a finish line, and out of all the instruments, the kick drum is the first one that crosses that line, and that's what makes people dance and move.

Up until that time I pretty much concentrated on my hands and flash, but I went and shedded all weekend and managed to secure some space on the record. If it wasn't for that, my name would have been on the record but John Molo would have played all the drums. I am forever indebted to Michael for that. I can honestly say that I don't think I would have made it as far as I have if I hadn't followed his instruction.

What kind of headphone mix do you prefer when you're recording?
It definitely varied and a lot of it depends on who I'm playing with. When I play with a great bass player like Paul ILL, I want to hear a lot of bass, but I've been known to record stuff where there's just vocals and click track.

Do you like recording that way?
I like to get in and get out of the studio because I feel that my moment of inspiration isn't long. Sometimes not everyone in the studio is going to have the same skill set. I tend to learn arrangements quickly and if there's someone in the band who doesn't learn as quickly or isn't inspired, or maybe really feels the pressure of the moment, that can slow everything down. That makes things a lot harder for me.

As a result, I usually adjust what I'm listening to in the first two or three takes and that's based on me not losing my window of inspiration and less based on everyone else. I want to capture the magic where you play things that you don't think about and it's just a pure unconscious reaction to the music you're listening to.

That's why I sometimes just listen to the click and vocal because I don't want to be distracted by anyone else. I'd prefer to have a foundation of the bass to record with, but if it's a question between that and having my window of inspiration, I'll pick the inspiration every time. On the other hand, sometimes I'll turn everyone up because it's just magic and it's what every drummer wants.

How long is that window?
It varies. Every single experience is different, so it's not really quantifiable. When I did all those Lynda Perry records she was all about that.

I don't know that I ever heard her call it the "inspired moment," but it was all done as quickly as possible. That wasn't because of being lazy and wanting to get out of there quickly, but because there's this fine space between reacting to the music where you don't really know where you're going, and knowing the song so well that you already know what you're going to play.

At Lynda's place you played five days a week and had to get it right, but you weren't allowed to think about it. You'd just react and be unconscious and inspired. Those two things create the perfect moment for me.

Do you have any advice for someone just starting out in the business?
Yeah, learn everything there is to know about the job. Don't be lazy and don't expect someone else to do all the work for you. It's one thing to be a talented player; it's another not to know anything about the business aspects that come along with it.

DAVE WECKL

Dave Weckl is truly one of the most widely respected drummers in the drumming world. From his early days with Chick Corea's Elektric Band, to touring with the likes of Simon and Garfunkel and Mike Stern, to playing on numerous radio and television jingles and soundtracks, to sessions with Robert Plant, George Benson, and Peabo Bryson (among many others), to being a highly regarded solo artist in his own right, Dave has always been recognized as a cutting-edge innovator of his instrument.

Dave is also a consummate educator, with many instructional videos/DVDs and play-along packages to his credit. You can learn a lot more about Dave and his instructional products at daveweckl.com.

Can you describe your kit for us?

I have a few kits, and what I use depends on the music that's going to be played. I've played and endorsed Yamaha drums since 1983, and I received my first Yamaha kit, a Recording Custom model, while on tour with Simon and Garfunkel.

Today, my standard kit for fusion, funk/jazz-rock situations is a five-piece Maple Custom with a vintage finish, with an extra snare to the left. It's composed of a 22"x16" kick, 8"x10", 8"x12", 12"x14", and 14"x16" toms, and a 5.5"x14" maple or aluminum snare, and a 5"x13" maple signature snare.

I'll also usually use a smaller 18"x16" bass drum for acoustic jazz gigs, usually with fewer toms as well. I've also helped to design cymbals for Sabian, the HHX Evolution, and Legacy lines to date, and I use a wide assortment of crashes, splashes, effects cymbals and rides, again, depending on the music to be played. I also use percussion accessories from LP, and my sticks are my signature series from Vic Firth.

What do you look for in a kit?

I look for warm, resonant, projecting shells that help me express what I am hearing in my head, with user-friendly hardware that's stable but not too bulky or heavy. The kit has to conform to me, not the other way around, meaning the drums and hardware have to be able to be adjusted in fine increments, and needs to stay put where it is. The kit has to feel right and sound right, and Yamaha has the build quality necessary for that to happen.

The drum seat and pedals are of utmost importance to feel good and work with the body. Again, Yamaha fits the bill with the Flying Dragon double pedal and very comfortable and stable drum seats.

Do you have a big drum collection?
I have a few vintage snares, but I'm not a collector by any means. I still have my very first Gretsch kit, a custom-made maple kit that I had in college, and about four or five different Yamaha kits, all of which are pretty old. I do have an authentic Buddy Rich Slingerland kit that he played in the '70s, though, complete with his logo bass drum head, and all heads signed by him and Sonny Payne.

Do you bring multiple kits or snares to a session?
I try to get as much info about the session ahead of time so I don't bring unnecessary gear. I usually end up bringing a couple different bass drums (small and big) and a couple different snares, but I bring lots of different cymbals to choose from.

Do you tailor the kit to the session?
Yes, always. It is important for me to know the style of music to be played before I get there.

How does your recording kit differ from your live kit?
It doesn't change at all. I use the same setup for live shows as I do in the studio.

Do you use bottom heads or a head on front of the kick drum?
I always use bottom heads on toms. The bass drum front head type will depend on the music, and whether I want a resonant or dead bass drum sound.

For the dead sound I port the front head at about four o'clock with about a 4" hole. If I play with a full front head, I usually punch small nail size holes about an inch or so in from the hoop at each lug to let some air out while still retaining the full resonant sound of the head and drum. I've also co-designed a muffling system for the bass drum with Remo that is part of my tuning formula for the sound of the kick drum.

What kind of heads do you use?
I use Remo heads. Generally I use coated Ambassadors on all tops of

all drums, including the bass drum, and clear Ambassadors on the bottoms of all toms.

How often do you do maintenance on your kit?
Yamaha kits don't need much maintenance, but I have a cartage/storage company that helps me with that task [Drum Paradise, Los Angeles], so I make sure that the kit is constantly in top form.

What are your favorite mics on your kit?
Again, this will depend on the music to be played and the general sound desired, but I endorse and use Shure mics and have done so for many years. My usual live and studio preference is a Beta 52 for the kick, SM-57s on snares, SM-98s on toms, KSM-141s for overheads, and an SM-81 for hats. I will also use the big condenser mics, like KSM-44s, on overheads if I want a bigger drum sound.

In the studio I'll use an identical setup, but sometimes add some very high end overhead mics, like the DPA (B&K) 4011s that I'm currently using. I also use the KSM-44s for room mics in the studio.

When you're recording, what do you like in your headphone mix?
Everything has to be in the phones, including all the drums, but the exact levels will depend on the players, the music, and whether or not there is a click or sequence.

What kind of headphones do you like?
I use the Shure E5 in-ear monitors (with black rubber ear pieces) for everything, live and in the studio.

Do you tune your drums yourself or do you hire someone like the Drum Doctor to do it?
No one tunes my drums but me. Ever!

How do you go about tuning your drums, then?
That, of course, depends on the music to be played. I usually start on the toms with the bottom head, get it in tune with itself, then tune the top head about a minor third lower. The pitch between toms is about a fourth apart most of the time. If mics are involved, I may have to work with the pitch and tuning to accommodate the room or the PA. My main snare is usually tuned medium high in pitch, but again will depend on

the music and desired sound. The bottom head is always tighter, and usually pretty tight in general. The bass drum I usually pitch very low.

Which drum do you start with?
I don't have a preference, but I usually start with the small tom and work my way down in size where the toms are concerned.

Do you tune to the resonant frequency of the drum?
Well, I've never understood how that could make sense for all situations, so I would say no. I tune to the pitch and decay factor that I want.

Do you ever adjust the tuning to the song?
Sometimes, especially the snare in a pop vocal song. I want the backbeat snare tone to be somewhat congruent with the song's tonal center.

Do you deaden any part of your kit with Moon Gel, Deadringers, or tape?
Sometimes. It will depend on the music and the effect I want to get. In general though, I don't deaden anything except maybe the kick a bit. I also designed an active muffler for the snare with Remo, which works like a physical noise gate. It's a felt-covered plunger that clamps onto the rim, which comes slightly off the drum on impact, then comes back down on the head to muffle it.

Do you have any advice for a young drummer just starting out?
You have to "want" to do this because it will take a lot of your time, dedication, and sacrifice to get good enough to succeed.

Any advice for someone just starting to record?
Yes, hang out with someone that does it a lot, because there is no substitute for watching, listening, and learning. Then, experiment.

What kind of gigs are the hardest for you?
Being involved with people that are not interested in making the situation work.

What do you hate about recording?
I hate being involved with unprofessional situations, like bad studios

where things don't work, incompetent engineers where things sound bad, and unprepared musicians.

What do you hate about drumming?
I hate the fact that one day it will take a toll on the body (well, that and just aging) to a point where I won't be able to express myself the way I want to on the drums.

GLOSSARY

attack: The first part of a sound. On a compressor/limiter, a control that affects how that device will respond to the attack of a sound.

attenuation: A decrease in level or volume.

bandwidth: The spectrum of frequencies that a device will pass before the signal degrades. A human being can supposedly hear from 20Hz to 20kHz, so the bandwidth of the human ear is 20Hz to 20kHz.

basic track: Recording the rhythm section for a record, which may be only the drums but would most likely include all the instruments of the band, depending upon the project. A point in the recording process before any overdubs, such as vocals, horns, strings, and percussion are added.

bass drum: Also known as the kick drum, it is the largest, lowest drum which sits sideways on the floor. In the early days of recording it was called the "foot drum" or "foot."

bell of a cymbal: The raised center section of the cymbal where its mounting hole is.

bi-directional: A microphone with a figure-8 pickup pattern, picking up equally on both the front and the back of the mic, yet rejecting the sound from its sides.

boom stand: A straight microphone stand with a pivoting arm attached that can be set at an angle.

bottom: Bass frequencies, the lower end of the audio spectrum. See also "low end."

bottom-end: See bottom.

buss: A signal pathway.

cable: Electrical cord to connect the mic to the recording console or pre-amplifier.

capsule: The part of a microphone that contains the primary electronic pickup element.

cardioid: A microphone that has a heart or kidney shaped pickup pattern. When a mic is set to cardioid position, it picks up sound primarily from the front of the mic.

channel: A track on a recording or one input on a recording console or mixing board.

clean: A signal with no distortion.

clip: To overload and cause distortion.

clipping: When an audio signal begins to distort because a circuit in the signal path is overloaded, the top of the waveform becomes "clipped" off and begins to look square instead of rounded. This usually results in some type of distortion, which can either be soft and barely noticeable, or horribly "crunchy" sounding.

close miking: Placing a mic close to an instrument in order to decrease the pickup of room reflections or other sound sources.

compression: Signal processing that controls and evens out the dynamics of a sound.

compressor: A signal processing device used to alter the audio dynamics.

condenser mic: A microphone that uses two electrically charged plates (thereby creating an electronic component known as a "condenser") as its basis of operation. Condenser microphones always employ on-board electronic circuitry to boost the signal to a usable level.

crash cymbal: A smaller cymbal frequently used to accent downbeats.

cue mix: The headphone mix sent to the musicians that differs from the one the producer and engineer are listening to.

cut: To decrease, attenuate, or make less.

DAW: Digital Audio Workstation. A computer loaded with the appropriate hardware and software needed to record and edit audio.

dB: Abbreviation for decibel, which is a unit of measurement of sound level.

deaden: To soften or reduce the "ringing" of an over-ambient room or instrument.

decay: the "falling off" portion of a sound from loud to silent. It also refers to the time it takes for a signal to fall below audibility.

decibel (dB): A unit of measurement of sound level or loudness.

diaphragm: The element of a microphone moved by sound pressure.

directional: A microphone that has most of its pickup pattern in one direction.

dynamic mic: A microphone that changes acoustic energy into electrical energy by the motion of a diaphragm through a magnetic field. A dynamic mic needs no additional on-board electronics to boost the signal.

dynamics: Variations in loudness and softness in a musical performance or audio signal.

edgy: A sound with an abundance of higher mid-range frequencies.

EQ: Equalizer, or to adjust an equalizer (tone control) to affect the timbral balance of a sound.

equalization: Adjustment of the frequency spectrum to even out or alter tonal imbalances.

equalizer: A tone control that can vary in sophistication from very simple to very complex (see parametric equalizer).

figure 8: A microphone with a pickup pattern primarily from the front and rear, with very little on the sides.

flip the phase: Engaging the phase switch on a console, preamp, or DAW channel in order to find the setting with the greatest bass response.

frequency: The speed of the vibration of a soundwave. Higher sounds vibrate faster than lower frequencies.

FS: Full scale. A digital peak meter that reads at 0 dB shows the full scale of the meter. It is the maximum amplitude of a digital system.

gain: The amount an audio signal is boosted.

gain reduction: The amount of compression or limiting.

gate: A signal-processing device which only allows audio to pass after a preselected volume level (threshold) is reached.

gated reverb: An effect used to cut off the decay of the reverb when it falls below a predetermined threshold.

groove: The pulse of the song and how the instruments dynamically breathe with it.

hardware (as in drum hardware): Cymbal stands and drum stands.

head: The "skin" stretched across a drum rim.

headroom: The amount of dynamic range between the normal operating level and the maximum level, which is usually the onset of clipping.

hertz: (Hz) The measurement unit of audio frequency, meaning the number of cycles per second. High numbers represent high sounds, and low numbers represent low sounds.

hi-hat: The two cymbals which "clap" together by means of a foot pedal.

high end: The high frequency response of a device.

high-pass filter: A frequency filter which allows only high frequencies to pass and rejects low frequencies. The frequency point where it cuts off is usually either switchable or variable.

Hz: Abbreviation for hertz.

input pad: An electronic circuit that attenuates the signal, usually 10 or 20 dB. See also "attenuation pad."

in the box: Doing all of your mixing with the software console in the Digital Audio Workstation application on the computer, instead of using an external hardware console.

iso booth: Short for isolation booth. It may also refer to an isolated section of the studio designed to eliminate sound leakage.

isolate: To separate one instrument from the others.

kick drum: See bass drum.

kHz: 1000 hertz (example: 4kHz = 4000Hz).

leakage: Sound from another instrument or sound source "bleeding" into a mic pointed at another instrument. It also refers to an acoustic spill from a sound source other than the one intended.

level/levels: Amount of audio volume.

limiter: A signal-processing device used to constrict or reduce audio dynamics, pushing down the loudest peaks in volume.

live room: A room with an abundance of audio reflections or echo.

low end: The lower end of the audio spectrum, or bass frequencies usually below 200Hz.

make-up gain: A control on a compressor/limiter that applies additional gain to the signal to compensate for the reduction in gain induced by the comp/limiter. This is required since the signal is automatically decreased when the compressor is working. Make-up gain "makes up" the gain and brings it back to where it was prior to being compressed.

mic: Short for microphone.

mic pad: See "pad."

midrange: Middle frequencies starting from around 250Hz up to 4000Hz.

mixing: Blending and combining different audio signals to mono, stereo, or surround sound.

monaural: A mix that contains a single channel and usually comes from only one speaker.

mono: Short for monaural, or single audio playback channel.

mute: An on/off switch. To mute something would mean to turn it off.

null: The point on the microphone pickup pattern where the pickup sensitivity is at its lowest.

off-axis: A sound source away from the primary pickup point of a microphone.

omnidirectional: A microphone that picks up sound equally from all sides.

ORTF: Acronym for the Office de Radiodiffusion Television Française; it is also a stereo-miking technique developed by the Office of French Radio and Television Broadcasting using two cardioid mics angled 110° apart and spaced seven inches (17 cm) apart horizontally.

overhead: The microphones placed above (over) the head of a drummer used either to pick up the entire kit, or just the cymbals.

overtones: A subtle, secondary quality of a sound that gives it its character.

pad: An electronic circuit that attenuates the signal (usually either 10 or 20dB) in order to avoid overload.

padding: Material used to control excessive overtones, ambience, or echo.

pan: Short for panorama—indicates the left and right position of an instrument in the stereo spectrum.

panning: Moving a sound across the stereo spectrum.

peaks: The loudest dynamic level of an audio signal compared to those around it.

phase: The relationship between two separate sound signals when combined into one.

phase shift: The process during which some frequencies (usually those below 100Hz) are slowed down ever so slightly as they pass through a device. This is usually exaggerated by excessive use of equalization creating a very slight (and undesirable) time lag.

pitch: An attribute of sound that varies with the frequency of a sound. It can also refer to the highness or lowness of a musical note.

preamp: An electronic circuit that boosts the low output of a microphone to a level that can be used by the other electronic devices in the studio.

presence: Accentuated upper mid-range frequencies in the 7–14kHz range.

pull: engineer slang meaning to remove or reduce.

punchy: A description for a quality of sound that infers good reproduction of dynamics with a strong impact. Sometimes means emphasis in the 200Hz and 5kHz areas.

push: Engineer slang meaning to add or increase.

range: On a gate or expander, a control that adjusts the amount of attenuation that will occur to the signal when the gate is closed. It can also refer to the dynamic spectrum of an audio signal or acoustic sound.

ratio: A parameter control on a compressor/limiter that determines how much compression or limiting will occur when the signal exceeds threshold.

release: The last part of a sound. On a compressor/limiter, it is the control that affects how that device will respond to the release of a sound.

resonant frequency: A particular frequency or band of frequencies that are emphasized, usually due to some extraneous acoustic, electronic, or mechanical factor.

reverb: A natural or artificially created echo or ambience that's used to simulate the sound of an environment, such as a room, a hall, or a church. It can also refer to a type of signal processor that reproduces the spatial sound of an environment (e.g., the sound of a closet or locker room or inside an oil tanker).

ribbon: A microphone that utilizes a thin aluminum ribbon as the main pickup element.

ride cymbal: The larger cymbal often used to keep tempo when playing a musical piece.

roll-off: Usually another word for high-pass filter, although it can also refer to a low-pass filter.

sibilance: A rise in the frequency response in a vocal where there's an excessive amount of 3–8kHz, resulting in the "s" sounds being overemphasized.

signal compression: See compression.

snare: A thin drum with springs or "strainers" underneath that create a "rattling" sound often used for the backbeat of a musical performance.

snare strainers: The string of springs on the bottom of the snare drum.

soundfield: The listening area containing mostly direct sound from the monitor speakers.

spectrum: The complete audible range of audio signals.

spot mic: A microphone used during orchestral recording to boost the level of an instrument or soloist.

stereo: Sound output coming from two speakers, resulting in a three-dimensional sound effect.

subgroup: A separate sub-mixer that sums selected assigned channels together, then sends that mix to the master mix buss.

sympathetic vibration: Vibrations, buzzes, and rattles or notes that occur in areas of an instrument, or other instruments, other than the one that was struck.

threshold: The point at which an effect takes place. On a compressor/limiter, the Threshold control adjusts the point at which compression will begin to occur.

throne: The drummer's chair.

tighter: Fewer overtones from a sound source, less acoustic decay.

timbre: Tonal color.

tom-tom (or just tom): Mid-sized drums on the floor, mounted on stands or attached to the bass drum.

track: A term sometimes used to mean a song. In recording, a separate musical performance that is recorded.

transient: A very short duration signal peak.

tuning: Adjusting the pitch to the desired musical note.

tunnel: A makeshift extension mounted to the front of a bass drum used to isolate a mic placed away from the drum head.

windscreen: A device placed over a microphone to attenuate the noise cause by wind interference.

X/Y: A stereo miking technique in which the microphone capsules are mounted as closely as possible while crossing at 90°.

INDEX